# Walk in the Spirit

*A Bible Study on the Holy Spirit of God*

Cara Smith

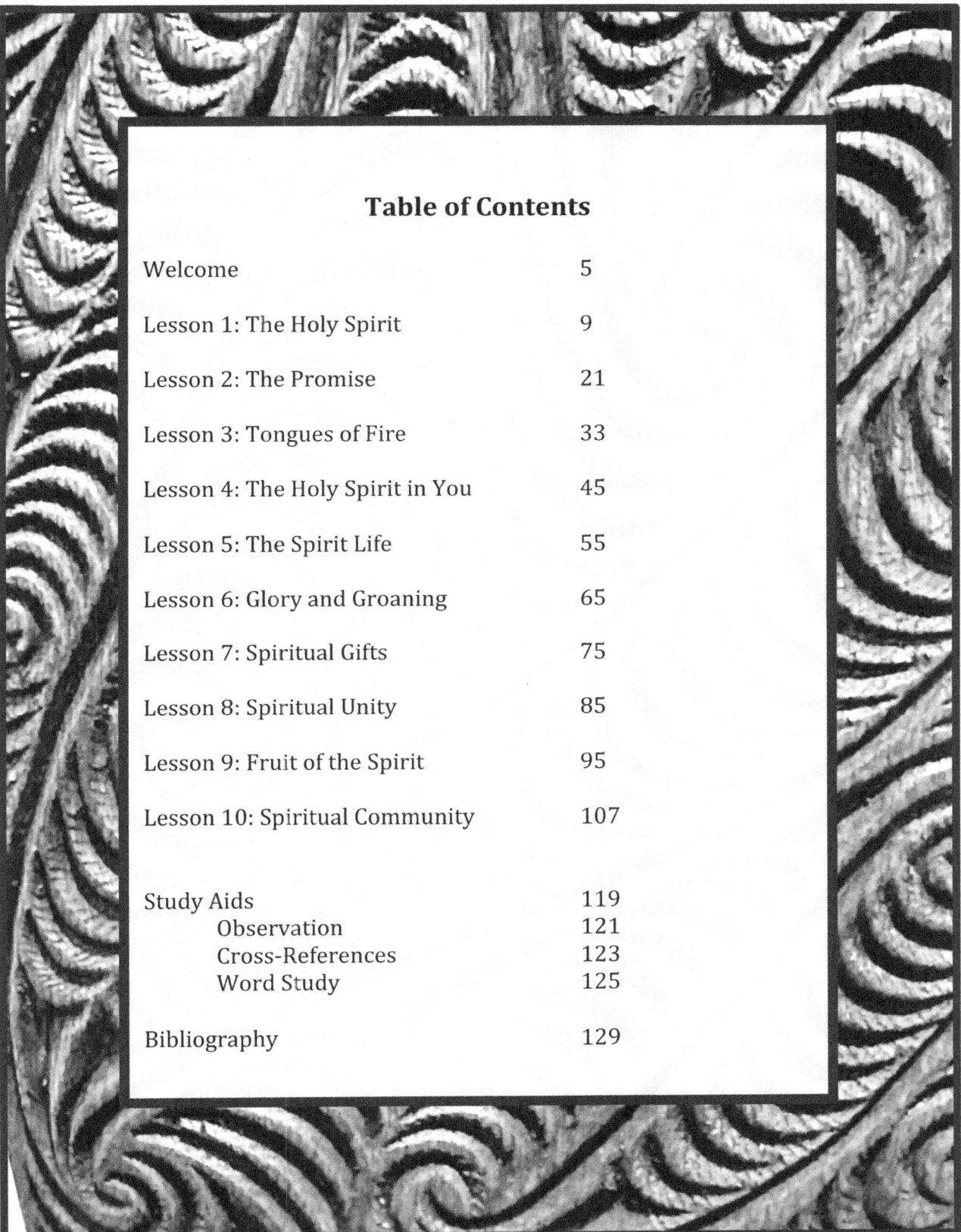

# Table of Contents

4

# Welcome

## Study Philosophy

Thanks for choosing *Walk in the Spirit: A Bible Study on the Holy Spirit of God.* This study is intended for a small group Bible study that values both in-depth personal study and lively group discussion. I am convinced that any believer can understand and apply the Bible to his or her own life by thorough personal preparation and group discussion.

Because the Bible is God's Word, it can speak to you in ways that other books do not. In 2 Timothy 3:16-17 it teaches that Scripture is "breathed out by God and profitable for teaching, for reproof, for correction and for training in righteousness, that the man of God may be competent, equipped for every good work" (ESV). Therefore, your personal interaction with Scripture is an interaction with God himself. By engaging with God, employing sound Bible study techniques, and developing consistent study habits, you can become a confident, competent Bible student. This kind of hands-on Bible study helps you not only master the text, but also lets the God who "breathed out" the text master you. It leads you to obedience, true life-change, and equips you for good work.

Once you have studied and interacted with the Scriptures for yourself, group discussion provides further insight and perspective. When each member has invested time in personal study, the discussion is informed and rich. But small group interaction is about much more than learning. When a group of believers meet with the Word of God as their focus, something else happens. They humbly engage with one another, providing encouragement, accountability, and the love it takes to live Christ-like, Spirit-directed, Bible-informed lives. They experience truth and love.

## Study Method

This Bible study is all about your relationship with the Holy Spirit. Because this study is topical, you will focus on several sections of Scripture. The first lesson is a survey of the nature and activity of the Holy Spirit. The fourth lesson is also a survey of how a person comes into relationship with the Holy Spirit through salvation. The other lessons will have one main passage to guide your thinking. These lessons are written from a guided inductive approach.

The questions are open-ended and require you to think for yourself. The study occasionally provides limited commentary and word definitions, but the purpose of this method is to guide discovery, not to provide teaching and answers. The inductive method includes observation, interpretation, and application questions.

Each numbered question of the study contains at least one type of question. Often, you will find that a numbered question uses several layered questions. These are meant to guide your thought process and often include more than one type of question. Understanding the types of questions will help you enter the inductive process and produce appropriate answers to the questions. To understand how to recognize observation, interpretation, and application questions, keep reading.

## Observation

Observation questions answer: *What does the text say?* Good observation leads you to look at the text objectively and factually. You'll know an observation question because it asks for a direct answer from the text. These questions bring out the "who, what, when, where, why, and how" of the passage. Sometimes there will be charts to fill out or lists to make that help you observe and organize the text. Try to keep from interpreting or applying as you answer these questions. Don't avoid these questions because they seem obvious or dismiss them as easy. Observation questions set the groundwork for later interpretation and application. After all, how can we decide what a passage means or how we should apply it to our lives if we haven't first closely observed what it says? (See more about this process in the *Observation* page in the Study Aids section at the end of the study.)

## Interpretation

Interpretation questions answer: *What does the text mean?* Cross-referencing, word studies, and examining context are all tools for understanding what the passage means to its fullest. Many of the questions will ask you to paraphrase or summarize what the text is saying. When you do this, you are interpreting. Some will ask directly what the passage means. This is a cue to use your cross-references and look up words even if the question doesn't provide them. (See more in the *Cross-reference* and *Word Study* pages in the Study Aids section.)

## Application

Application questions answer: *What should I do?* Application questions are open-ended and could have many different answers. They are meant to be probing and personal. Sometimes they will be encouraging; at other times they will be convicting or challenging. Always, they are meant to spur you to action! All three types of questions are important, but application is the ultimate goal of Bible study. We must be doers of the Word, not merely hearers (James 1:22). Don't skip these questions! Pray, ponder, and open yourself up to the work of God as you think through the application questions.

Sometimes you will discover your own applications or ask your own questions. This is great and a vital part of the inductive process. Ask and answer your own questions!

## Daily Exercises

Starting in the second lesson you will find a page titled *Daily Exercise*. This page is placed after the lesson's introduction page, before the main body of the Bible study for that week. The purpose of these exercises is to help you learn to relate to the Holy Spirit in deeper and more practical ways. You will be invited to do each exercise daily during the week. No matter how you decide to tackle the homework for each week, take time to give some attention each day to the week's *Daily Exercise*. In discussion time you will process how the *Daily Exercise* impacted you with the rest of your group.

## Resource Guidelines

This study is written using the *English Standard Version* (ESV) of the Bible. You will need a good translation of the Bible with faithfulness to the original Greek and Hebrew texts. ESV, NASB or NIV translations with cross-references will work for this study. "Living" translations or paraphrases like *The Message* are valuable for devotional reading but are not best for this type of inductive study.

You will occasionally need an English dictionary or a Greek expository dictionary such as *The Complete Word Study Dictionary – New Testament* by Spiros Zodhiates. (See the Bibliography for more resources.) Bible websites such as *blueletterbible.org* and apps such as *Literal Word* also provide resources for word study. (See *Word Study* in the *Study Aids* section for more information.)

You will not need commentaries for this study, but feel free to consult commentaries and the study notes in your Bible *after* you have done your homework. Scholarship is good and is to be utilized only after you have done your own work at understanding a passage. It is just too easy to shortcut study by going immediately to commentaries. It prevents your development as a student and deprives you of the thrill of personal discovery that you get when you have worked through a passage for yourself. There are also some trusted resources in the Bibliography.

## How to Use This Study

Complete one lesson per week. It will take *at least* two hours of personal study to complete a lesson. Try to do the *Daily Exercise* each day. Don't be discouraged if you don't reach that goal. Any time spent in the *Daily Exercise* would be a valuable part of your growth as a follower of Jesus indwelt by God's Spirit.

It will take a group one and a half to two hours to discuss a lesson and have time to worship and pray for one another. The most logical flow for discussion is to do the questions in numerical order. You may want to move more quickly through the observation questions since they are typically more objective. This leaves plenty of time for discussion when interpretation and application questions come. Don't feel compelled to discuss every question. Sometimes a group will profit by focusing on a certain aspect of the study, depending on the needs of the group, so flexibility can be good. Try to avoid going too far off topic. "Rabbit trails" are usually counter-productive and frustrating for most members of the group.

# Lesson 1

# The Holy Spirit

The goal of our study over the next ten weeks is to deepen both our understanding and our experience of what it means to truly live under the influence of the Holy Spirit. To reach this goal, or to at least start the process of reaching this goal, we must come to know the Holy Spirit as the Bible presents him.

The New Testament teaches the Christian to live his or her life controlled by the Holy Spirit. It describes this intertwined relationship with exhortations to walk with the Spirit, keep in step with the Spirit, set our minds on the Spirit, and be filled with the Spirit. If we are going to relate to the Holy Spirit in these ways, we must start by understanding his true nature.

So, to begin our journey, let's survey the main ways that the Bible describes the Holy Spirit.

In this lesson we will:
- Consider the Holy Spirit's personhood and his deity.
- Establish the connection between the Father, Son, and Spirit.
- Consider the names the Bible uses for the Holy Spirit.
- Compile a list of the Holy Spirit's ministries.
- Contemplate the word pictures the New Testament uses to describe the Holy Spirit.

Because this lesson is a survey of doctrine it may seem a little academic, but don't let it be! As you understand more of the Holy Spirit's true nature, open yourself up to him as if you were having that first deep "get to know you" conversation with him.

## The Holy Spirit is a Person

When we use the word "person," it usually means a human being. When Christian theologians teach about personhood, they mean something different. In hymns and creeds, you have heard that God exists in three persons. Used this way, "person" means a spiritual being that has an *intellect, a will, and emotions.*[1] Angels, demons, Satan, humans, and God are all persons. God's uniqueness comes from the fact that he exists as one God in three persons: the Father, Son, and Holy Spirit. Each person of the trinity is fully God, unique from the others, and yet they co-exist as one essence in unity.

[1] MacArthur Jr., John F. and Mayhue, Richard, *Biblical Doctrine A Systematic Summary of Bible Truth.* Wheaton, IL: Crossway, 2017.

1. To immerse yourself in the truth of the Holy Spirit's personhood, look up each of these references and determine how the Holy Spirit is exercising his *will, intellect,* and/or *emotion.* What is the Holy Spirit doing in each? (We will fully consider the implications of each of these activities in future studies, so don't draw any applications or additional interpretation yet.)

Example:
Isaiah 11:2
The Holy Spirit rests upon the "shoot from the stump of Jesse" and gives him wisdom, knowledge, understanding, counsel, might, and the fear of Yahweh. (He uses his *will* to rest upon the future Messiah in this prophecy. He uses his *intelligence* to give wisdom etc.)

John 14:26


Acts 1:16


Acts 8:29


Romans 5:5


1 Corinthians 12:11


Ephesians 4:30


1 Thessalonians 1:6

2.  When the Bible uses a personal pronoun for the Holy Spirit, it never uses "it" or "she." The Holy Spirit, like the Father and Son is referred to as "he." This points to the unity of God, but it also debunks some common misconceptions about the Holy Spirit. For example, the Holy Spirit is not an impersonal power source we plug into to get extra power to accomplish our goals. What are some other analogies you may have heard about the Holy Spirit? How do they confirm or deny his personhood?

3.  If the Holy Spirit is a person, that means he relates to us, as believers, personally. As you begin this study, try to describe your relationship with the Holy Spirit. How do you currently relate to him? What is this experience like for you? (This question is meant to help you identify a starting place to gauge your growth over the next ten weeks.)

## The Trinity

The concept of a God who is one God yet existing and functioning as three persons is a mystery. No other person has this triune nature. Therefore, as we move forward in our understanding of the Holy Spirit we must cling to the truth of Scripture and think with restraint and humility. We must not add our opinions to what the Scripture says or attempt our own illustrations to simplify the mystery of one God in three persons. One place to begin to understand the relationship between the Father, Son, and Spirit is to see how they related at various times in biblical history.

4.  Carefully observe and summarize what these passages say about the cooperative activity of the Father, Son, and Holy Spirit.

In creation (Genesis 1:2, 1:26; John 1:1-3; and Colossians 1:15-17).

Surrounding Jesus' birth (Luke 1:34-35; Luke 2:25-27).

At Jesus' baptism (Matthew 3:13-17; John 1:32-33).

At Jesus' temptation in the desert (Matthew 4:1-4).

At Jesus' atoning death (Hebrews 9:13-14).

Causing Jesus' resurrection (John 10:17-18 and Romans 1:4; 8:11).

When Jesus commissioned his disciples (Matthew 28:18-20).

When sending the Holy Spirit to the disciples and the church (John 16:7; Acts 1:4-5; Acts 2:36-38).

5. God is one essence but three persons. This is not only difficult for us to understand but also confusing as we relate to God. When we pray, worship, or think of God, we may gravitate toward reducing him to one of his persons. Do you relate more strongly to the Father, Son, or Spirit? If so, which one and why? How do you think you could open yourself up to more of God's triune nature as you pray and worship?

## The Holy Spirit's Names

The Bible gives the Holy Spirit many names. Some of these names are in relationship to the Father or the Son and some refer only to the Spirit. By contemplating this list, you can see his character and relationship with the other members of the trinity more fully. Ponder this list and then answer the questions that follow (no need to look up the references).

### The Holy Spirit and the Father

His Spirit (Num. 11:29; Rom. 8:11)
Your Spirit (Ps. 139:7)
Your Holy Spirit (Ps. 51:11)
The Promise of the Father (Acts 1:4)
The Spirit of God (Gen. 1:2; Matt. 3:16; 1 Cor. 2:11)
The Spirit of the living God (2 Cor. 3:3)
The Spirit of your Father (Matt. 10:20)
The Spirit of the LORD (Judg. 3:10)
The Spirit of the Lord (Luke 4:18)
The Spirit of the Lord GOD (Isa. 61:1)

### The Holy Spirit and the Son

The Spirit of Jesus (Acts 16:7)
The Spirit of Christ (Rom. 8:9; 1 Pet. 1:11)
The Spirit of Jesus Christ (Phil. 1:19)
The Spirit of the Lord (Acts 5:9; 8:39)
The Spirit of his Son (Gal. 4:6)

### The Holy Spirit

The Spirit (Num. 11:17; Matt. 4:1)
The Eternal Spirit (Heb. 9:14)
Your Good Spirit (Ps. 143:10)
The Holy Spirit (Matt. 1:18)
One Spirit (Eph. 4:4)

6. What do you notice about these names? What can you infer about the relationship between the Father, Son, and Spirit? How does this help you understand the Holy Spirit better?

**Titles That Include Attributes**

The Spirit of counsel and might (Isa. 11:2)
The Spirit of faith (2 Cor. 4:13)
The Spirit of glory (1 Pet. 4:14)
The Spirit of grace (Heb. 10:29; cf. Zech. 12:10)
The Spirit of holiness (Rom. 1:4)
The Spirit of knowledge and the fear of the LORD (Isa. 11:2)
The Spirit of life (Rom. 8:2)
The promised Holy Spirit (Eph. 1:13)
The Spirit of truth (John 14:17; 15:26; 16:13; 1 John 4:6)
The Spirit of wisdom and of revelation in the knowledge of him (Eph. 1:17)
The Spirit of wisdom and understanding (Isa. 11:2)
The Helper (John 14:26; 15:26; 16:7)

7. Consider these titles and write a description of the Holy Spirit's character.

8. Consider these titles and write a description of what the Holy spirit can give to a believer. What is his ministry based on these titles? (There is more to his ministry than these titles suggest, but it is a good place to start.)

## The Holy Spirit's Ministries

9. As we continue our survey of what the Bible teaches about the Holy Spirit, we are going to compile a list of his *ministries*. We won't look at each of these deeply yet since we are just trying to get the big picture of the Holy Spirit's identity and activity. As you look up these references summarize only what you find out about the Holy Spirit's *work*. (Again, we will study these passages in future lessons, so don't look for applications yet.)

John 14:15-17, 26

John 16:7-11



Acts 1:8



Acts 2:4



Acts 4:8-12



Acts 13:2-4



Romans 8:9-11



Romans 8:13



Romans 8:14-16



Romans 8:26-27

1 Corinthians 2:9-16


1 Corinthians 6:11


1 Corinthians 12:4-13


2 Corinthians 1:22; 5:5


Galatians 5:16-18


Galatians 5:22-25


Galatians 6:6-8


Ephesians 1:13-14

Ephesians 4:1-6

Ephesians 5:18-20

Philippians 3:3

Titus 3:4-7

1 Peter 1:2

1 Peter 4:14

10. What surprised you as you considered these scriptures? What new insight did you gain? What questions arose? (Questions and a curious mindset will help you as you study in the coming weeks.)

## Word Pictures for the Holy Spirit

The Old Testament, roughly two thirds of the Bible, has about eighty references to the Holy Spirit. The New Testament, though much smaller, has almost two hundred fifty references to the Holy Spirit. The Bible uses eight main metaphors to describe the Holy Spirt and his work: The Holy Spirit is like clothing, a dove, fire, oil, a pledge, a seal, water, and wind. Of these, only water and wind appear in the Old Testament but all eight are in the New Testament. (These metaphors are also used elsewhere to describe very different things, so we need to be careful, when we encounter these metaphors, and use context to determine meaning. For example, fire is used to signify judgment as well as the Holy Spirit.)

11. For each of these metaphors, read the references included and try to discern why that particular metaphor or symbol was an appropriate comparison for the Holy Spirit. In what way is the Holy Spirit (a person) similar to the object? (Use a commentary or your study Bible's notes if necessary.)

Clothing
(Luke 24:49)

Dove
(Matthew 3:16; Luke 3:22; John 1:32)

Fire
(Acts 2:3)

Oil/Anointing
(2 Corinthians 1:21-22; 1 John 2:20,27)

A Pledge or Guarantee
(2 Corinthians 1:22; Ephesians 1:14)

A Seal
(2 Corinthians 1:22; Ephesians 1:13; 4:30)


Water
(John 7:38-39; Acts 1:5; 2:33; 1 Corinthians 12:13; Titus 3:5-6)


Wind
(John 3:8; Acts 2:2)


12. Look back at each of these metaphors and consider that you can experience the Holy Spirit in these ways. Which of these particularly enhances your understanding of how you could experience the Holy Spirit? Why?


13. End your study this week by writing a prayer of worship and by asking the Holy Spirit to open your mind to the fullness of his nature and work.

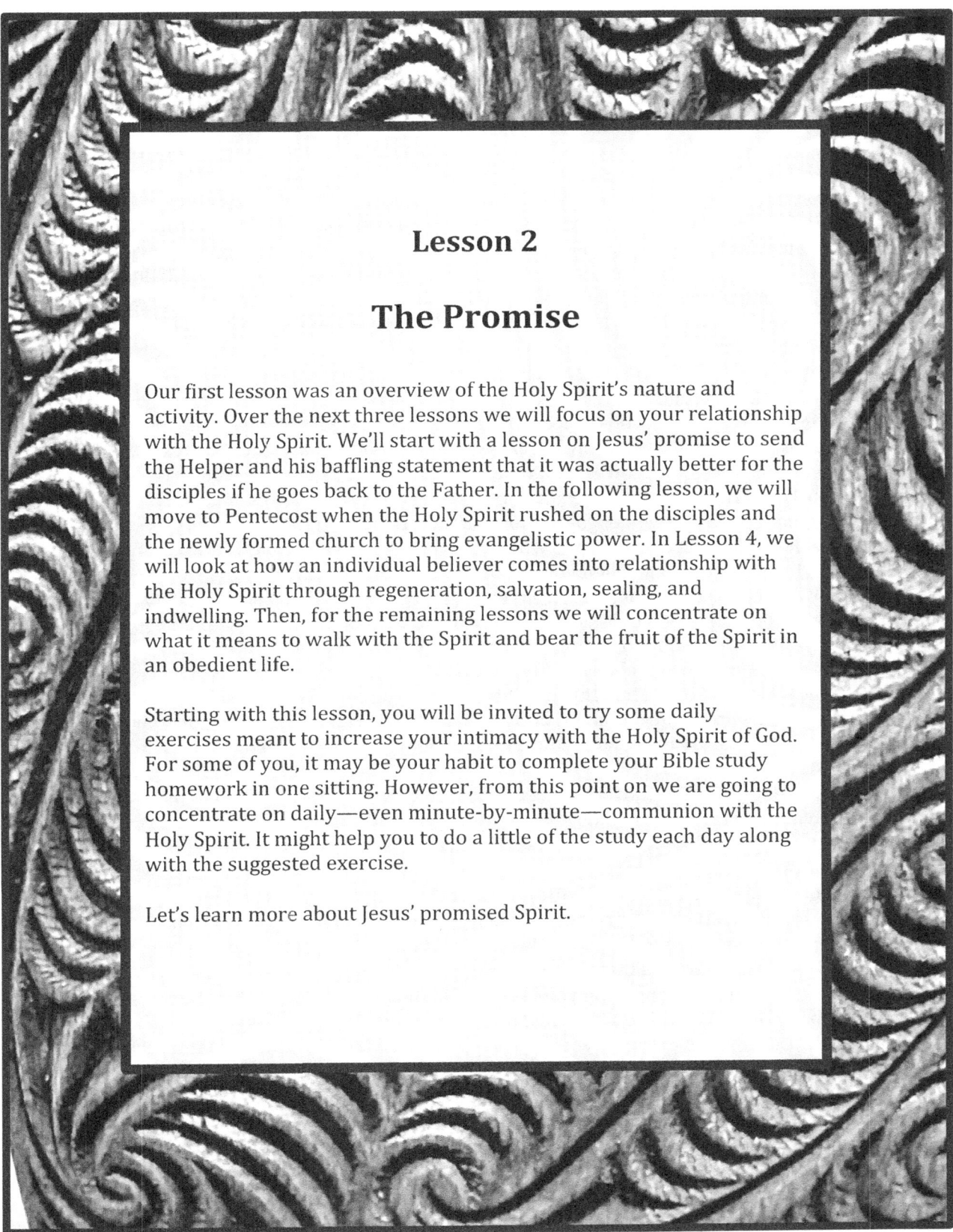

# Lesson 2

# The Promise

Our first lesson was an overview of the Holy Spirit's nature and activity. Over the next three lessons we will focus on your relationship with the Holy Spirit. We'll start with a lesson on Jesus' promise to send the Helper and his baffling statement that it was actually better for the disciples if he goes back to the Father. In the following lesson, we will move to Pentecost when the Holy Spirit rushed on the disciples and the newly formed church to bring evangelistic power. In Lesson 4, we will look at how an individual believer comes into relationship with the Holy Spirit through regeneration, salvation, sealing, and indwelling. Then, for the remaining lessons we will concentrate on what it means to walk with the Spirit and bear the fruit of the Spirit in an obedient life.

Starting with this lesson, you will be invited to try some daily exercises meant to increase your intimacy with the Holy Spirit of God. For some of you, it may be your habit to complete your Bible study homework in one sitting. However, from this point on we are going to concentrate on daily—even minute-by-minute—communion with the Holy Spirit. It might help you to do a little of the study each day along with the suggested exercise.

Let's learn more about Jesus' promised Spirit.

### *Daily Exercise One*: Worshipful Connection

In John 4:10, 13-14 Jesus invited the woman at the well to seek the living water that wells up to eternal life. (In John 7:37-39 Jesus makes it clear that the living water was the Holy Spirit.) In John 4:23-24 as Jesus continues his conversation with the woman at the well, he shares profound truth about God's nature and the practice of worshipful connection. He tells her that God is spirit and those who worship must worship in spirit and in truth. In other words, because God is a spiritual being we must worship him by engaging our spirits with his. As we do this, we must make sure we are worshipping him as he has presented himself in the Word of God (in truth). We will learn more about the Holy Spirit's indwelling presence and ministry in the life of a believer in future lessons. Therefore, before you begin this exercise, it is helpful to know that the moment you believed in the saving work of Jesus, you were permanently indwelled by the Holy Spirit. The Holy Spirit is already in you. This exercise will just help you acknowledge this reality in a worshipful way.

Every day this week consider entering into a time of personal worship and connection. To focus on God's *true* character, find a scripture about God's character. You will use this later in the exercise. Some good choices would be Exodus 34:6-7; Psalms 29, 100, or 103; and Revelation 1:17-18, but you can use any scripture that describes God's character.

To make sure that you engage your spirit with God's Spirit, try this approach: Close your eyes and try to remember a time when you knew for certain that God was communicating with you. This may be a time when you found comfort in physical, relational, or emotional pain. It could be a circumstance when you were undeniably convicted of sin or strongly led in a certain direction by God. It could be a time when you experienced unexplainable joy (possibly in the midst of trial). It could be a time when you very tangibly knew that God loved you. The point is to remember an actual encounter that you had with God in the past.

Once you have identified this past life experience, try to remember as much as you can about it and relive it in your mind. What did you sense in your body? What did you feel in your emotions? What did you think with your mind? Who was there with you? What were your physical surroundings?

Now that you have thoroughly remembered this experience, begin to pray, and tell God all about what you remember (like you would tell a friend). Thank him for the way he met you in the past and praise him for all the aspects of his character that you experienced in this circumstance.

Now that you are in conversation with God, continue to praise him using your scripture for this morning. Keep praising and thanking him. This would also be a good time to sing a favorite hymn of praise or to listen to a favorite worship song. (The Chapel in Akron has a Spotify playlist. Consider making your own worship playlist for the future.)

As you have been engaging your spirit with God's Spirit, what else has come to mind? Is there a sin to confess? Is there a circumstance in your life that you need to process with the Holy Spirit? Continue to pour out your life to God and ask the Holy Spirit to interact with your spirit to help you pray according to God's will.

As you finish your worship and connection time, consider asking the Father, Son, and Spirit to reveal themselves to you as you seek to love and obey them in all things today. Ask for the power and fellowship of the Holy Spirit for today's activities.

This exercise was informed by the teaching in *The Other Half of Church* by Jim Wilder and Michel Hendricks. See Bibliography.

## Where are You Going?

Let's turn our attention to a very specific time and place in history. On the night before Jesus was crucified, he had an intimate dinner with his disciples. The crowds were gone, and Jesus had prepared a private place to celebrate the Passover with his friends. He loved his disciples by washing their feet. He broke bread with them and passed the cup instituting the communion of remembrance. He sent out Judas, his betrayer, and he predicted the way Peter would deny him and the others would scatter. Then, he began to teach that he was going to prepare a place for them—a place where they could not immediately follow him. The disciples were confused and began to question him. In this context, Jesus taught about the Helper whom he would send and about the unity between himself, the Father, and the Holy Spirit.

Read John 14:1-26. As you read, pay attention to the relationship between the Father, Son, and Spirit. This will prepare you to think about Jesus' teaching on this last evening of his life.

1. In John 14:1-7 what is Thomas confused about? How does Jesus answer his question? What does Jesus teach about the connection between the Father and the Son?

2. In John 14:8-11 what is Philip confused about? What is Jesus' emotion as he answers? What does Jesus want Philip to believe?

3.  Review John 14:1-11 and make a list of everything Jesus teaches about his relationship to the Father. Why is it crucial for the disciples to know this on the eve of Jesus' crucifixion?

4.  In John 14:12-13 Jesus tells the disciples what they will do after he leaves. What does he mean when he says his disciples will do the works that he does? What does he mean when he says they will do greater works? What makes the works greater?

5.  In what way does Jesus' departure to the Father facilitate these works?

6. The phrase "in my name" appears twice in John 14:13-14. To pray "in Jesus' name" does not mean to tack this phrase on the end of any request we make. It is not a formula for prayer. Jesus' "name" is meant to point to his character, teaching, example, commandments, and will. With this in mind, what does it mean that Jesus will do whatever is asked in his name? What are the limits to the promise in John 14:14?

7. Consider your normal prayers. What changes could you make so that you pray more in line with Jesus' character, teaching, example, commandments, and will? How might this cause the Father to be glorified in the Son, as it says in John 14:14?

## Commandments and Love

8. So far, Jesus has told his disciples to believe (14:1,11). He has told them they will do his works and greater works than him (14:12). He has invited them to pray in his name (14:14). Next, Jesus tells them that if they love him, they will keep his commandments (14:15). He will explain more about the connection between love and commandment keeping soon, but before he does, he introduces the Holy Spirit. Make a list of everything you learn about the Holy Spirit from John 14:16-17.

9.  In the context of everything Jesus has taught so far, what does it mean that the Holy Spirit will be a helper? What will the Holy Spirit help us with?

10. How long will the Holy Spirit help? Why does this matter?

11. In John 14:17 it becomes clear that every person will not receive the Holy Spirit. Who will and won't have the Spirit? Where will the Spirit be in relationship to a believer?

12. Read John 14:18-24 and pay careful attention to the relationship between love for Jesus and keeping his commands. How do these two things relate?

13. How have you seen love for Jesus affect your desire to obey? How has your obedience or disobedience affected your love for Jesus? What can you do to grow in love and obedience?

14. Now read John 14:18-26 again and pay attention to the relationship between the Father, the Son, and a believer. Make some observations from the passage about how a believer grows close to God. What does it mean that the Father and Son will come and make their home with a believer (John 14:23)?

15. When have you sensed closeness to God most tangibly? When have you felt distant? What made the difference?

16. How is the Holy Spirit involved in your desire and practice of love and obedience? What does he do to help (John 14:17,23,26)?

17. What is some evidence that the triune God has made his home with you? Think of at least three.

## Bearing Witness

18. In John 15:18-25 Jesus warns his disciples of what is to come for them. Summarize the warnings in this section. Who will hate them and why?

19. At the end of these warnings Jesus teaches additional important truth about the Holy Spirit. Read John 15:26. What more do you learn about the Holy Spirit's relationship with the Father and the Son? What will the Holy Spirit do according to John 15:26?

20. What will the disciples do according to John 15:27? What does this mean? (Consider what Jesus says in Matthew 28:16-20 after his resurrection.)

21. What will be the reaction to this witness according to John 16:1-4? Why this reaction?

22. Why does Jesus warn them about this?

23. Why is it important to remember that a primary activity of the Holy Spirit is his witness to the truth of Jesus? How could this change the way you interact with the Holy Spirit?

24. How could you pray in Jesus' name about your witness to others? (Think about awareness, opportunity, preparation to speak, and particular people.)

25. Stop and write a prayer asking for help from the Holy Spirit to be a witness about Jesus.

## The Advantage

Remember, this whole body of teaching from Jesus is coming on the night before his crucifixion. By now the disciples have left the upper room (John 14:31) and they are walking to the garden of Gethsemane. Jesus continues to teach them as he is literally on the road to his betrayal and the cross.

26. In John 16:7 Jesus returns to direct teaching about the Holy Spirit. What surprising statement does Jesus make? Why could this be true according to John 16:8?

27. What does it mean that the Holy Spirit will convict the world concerning sin, righteousness, and judgment? (Use your cross references and commentary along with Jesus' explanations.)

Sin

Righteousness

Judgment

28. Jesus makes it clear that the world is not the enemy. The Holy Spirit was sent to help believers witness to the truth of Jesus and to convict the world so that unbelievers will have a change of heart and turn to Jesus. In this context, what does the Holy Spirit help the believer do? Why is the coming of the Holy Spirit an advantage to a believer? Why is the coming of the Holy Spirit an advantage to an unbeliever?

29. In John 16:12-15 Jesus describes another advantage that comes through the Holy Spirit after he returns to the Father. What will the Holy Spirit do?

30. What is "truth" in this context? Think of at least three ways the Holy Spirt will guide the disciples into truth.

31. Whose authority does the Holy Spirit have? Describe the relationship between the Father, Son, and Spirit.

32. Who gets glory as truth is revealed according to John 16:14? Why is this important for the understanding of truth?

33. Review this lesson and write a prayer asking the Helper to guide you into all truth so that you might increase in love for Jesus, obedience, and powerful gospel witness.

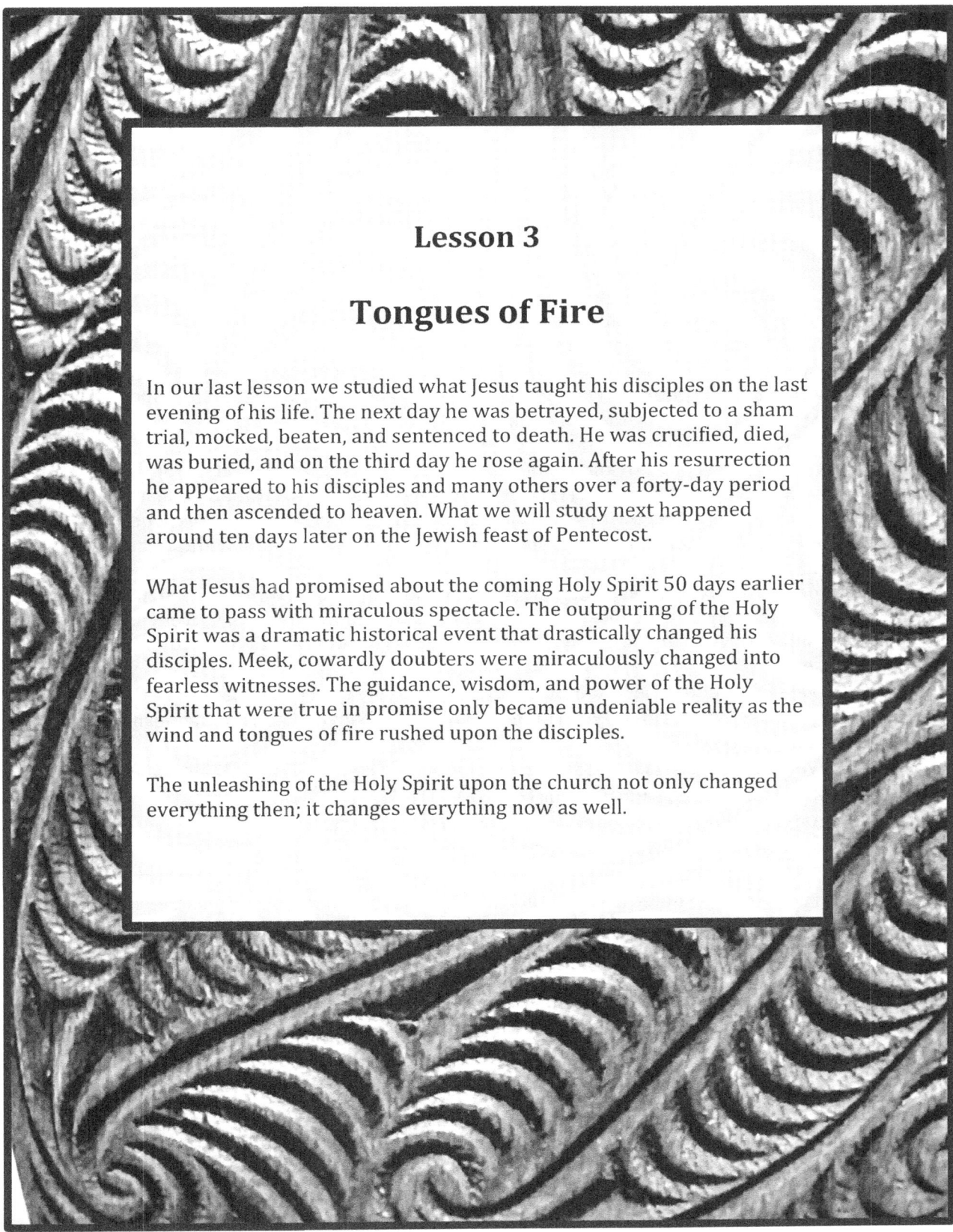

# Lesson 3

# Tongues of Fire

In our last lesson we studied what Jesus taught his disciples on the last evening of his life. The next day he was betrayed, subjected to a sham trial, mocked, beaten, and sentenced to death. He was crucified, died, was buried, and on the third day he rose again. After his resurrection he appeared to his disciples and many others over a forty-day period and then ascended to heaven. What we will study next happened around ten days later on the Jewish feast of Pentecost.

What Jesus had promised about the coming Holy Spirit 50 days earlier came to pass with miraculous spectacle. The outpouring of the Holy Spirit was a dramatic historical event that drastically changed his disciples. Meek, cowardly doubters were miraculously changed into fearless witnesses. The guidance, wisdom, and power of the Holy Spirit that were true in promise only became undeniable reality as the wind and tongues of fire rushed upon the disciples.

The unleashing of the Holy Spirit upon the church not only changed everything then; it changes everything now as well.

## *Daily Exercise Two*: Memorization

Remember, in our last lesson, Jesus taught that the Holy Spirit is our helper as we seek to obey Jesus' commands. One of the Holy Spirit's jobs is to bring to mind the truth of Jesus' teachings. In 1 Corinthians 2:10-16 it teaches us that the Holy Spirit searches the depths of God and reveals spiritual wisdom to believers. This wisdom is not worldly wisdom, but spiritual wisdom that can only be understood by those who are indwelt by the Holy Spirit. In 1 Corinthians 2:16 it tells us that this wisdom gives us the "mind of Christ."

What is this spiritual wisdom? In 2 Timothy 3:16 it tells us that, "All Scripture is breathed out by God and profitable for teaching, for reproof, for correction, and for training in righteousness, that the man of God may be competent, equipped for every good work." In 2 Peter 1:20-21 it adds, "knowing this first of all, that no prophecy of Scripture comes from someone's own interpretation. For no prophecy was ever produced by the will of man, but men spoke from God as they were carried along by the Holy Spirit."

Scripture is the source of truth and wisdom, and therefore, it is often what the Spirit brings to mind as he helps us to walk in obedience. It easily follows that if we want to walk in the Spirit, we will cooperate with the Spirit by studying the Word, listening the Word preached, and bringing the Word to mind all throughout the day in memorization and meditation.

Consider doing this exercise each day this week: Choose one verse or passage to memorize and meditate on this week. (Just choose one. You want to start slowly to have success and really let the verse sink into your thinking.) Here are some ideas of options with my favorites in parentheses:
- A verse that addresses a temptation you commonly face. (Ephesians 4:29-32)
- A passage that has given you comfort in the past that you have not memorized yet. (Philippians 4:4-7)
- A verse that describes God's or Jesus' character. (Psalm 107:8-9; Philippians 2:6-11)
- Part of a favorite psalm. (Psalm 103:1-5)
- A passage that encapsulates the gospel message. (Ephesians 2:8-10)
- The fruit of the Spirit. (Galatians 5:22-25)

Write this verse on two notecards. Put one notecard in your Bible to be rehearsed each morning as you pray and read the Bible. Put the second notecard somewhere that you will encounter it later in the day, such as the car, kitchen windowsill, or your purse/wallet.

Write out the verse and each day erase one or more of the words. The next time you rehearse the verse you will fill in the erased words from memory, then erase more words as you succeed.

Use some other visual cue to rehearse the verse during your day or read it and think about the truth contained in the verse. For example, when you drive past a certain landmark each day use it as a cue to think about this verse or talk to God about it.

Ask the Holy Spirit to spontaneously bring this verse to mind in your day.

## The Coming Spirit

1. The Bible records two separate occasions when Jesus talked to his disciples about the Holy Spirit after he had risen from the dead. The first is in John 20:19-22. When does this conversation happen? Where were the disciples and what was their emotional state? What does Jesus do and say in verses 19-20?

2. In this context, he says two important things in John 20:21. What does he say, and why does he say this now?

3. In John 20:22 Jesus breathed and told his disciples to "receive the Holy Spirit." We know that the disciples did not immediately begin going out to evangelize. They returned to their previous jobs and remained confused as to what they should do next. They also didn't demonstrate any new Holy Spirit-given power or understanding. Remember, Jesus declared in John 16:7 that he had to leave for the Holy Spirit to come to the disciples. All of this would suggest that when Jesus told them to receive the Holy Spirit, he was continuing to prophesy what was yet to come—but surely would come—after he ascended to heaven. Assuming that they didn't receive the Holy Spirit's permanent, indwelling power at that instant, why would Jesus remind them of the promise of the Holy Spirit then? How does the Holy Spirit relate to peace for the disciples and the fact that Jesus was sending them out to witness?

## Waiting

4. At the end of Luke's gospel, Luke records Jesus' second teaching about the Holy Spirit after Jesus' resurrection. What instruction does Luke 24:45-49 record?

5. In Acts 1:1-3 how does Luke describe Jesus' teaching? What part does the Holy Spirit play here?

6. In Acts 1:4-5 it repeats Jesus' instructions by recalling the image of baptism from early in Jesus' ministry. To baptize literally means to immerse. John the Baptist immersed people in water to symbolize the reality of repentance. What baptism is coming? With whom will believers be immersed soon? (Read John 1:32-34.)

7. The disciples are still confused about their mission. In Acts 1:6 what do the disciples ask? Why do they ask this? What is their expectation?

8. How does Jesus answer them in Acts 1:7-8? What should be their focus from now on? What part will the Holy Spirit play in this mission? (We will discuss this more later in the lesson.)

9. In Acts 1:9-11 what happens after Jesus tells them they will receive power when the Holy Spirit comes on them and that they will be witnesses of Jesus to the people around them? Why do you think these are Jesus' last instructions to them? (Remember Matthew 28:18-20.)

10. Why do the men in white robes speak to them? Why is this important information now?

11. While the disciples waited, they gathered in Jerusalem returning to an upper room. According to Acts 1:12-14, who was there and what were they doing?

12. In Acts 1:15-19 Peter describes something the Holy Spirit had done in ages past through David; what was this? What was Peter's and the disciples' response to this prophecy according to Acts 1:20-26?

13. How might this reaction to the Holy Spirit's voice in Old Testament prophecy prepare them for their mission? What pattern of obedience and prayer are they pursuing even before the Holy Spirit comes at Pentecost?

## Pentecost

The Jewish feast of Pentecost came fifty days after the Passover. This feast was a harvest festival also called the Feast of Weeks. It was a celebration with feasting, grain sacrifices, and animal sacrifices. These sacrifices were meant as an offering of first fruits to the Lord (Exodus 34:22-23). After the exile to Babylon ended and the Jewish people returned to Jerusalem, Jewish people also considered the Feast of Weeks to be a celebration of the giving of the Mosaic law. Ironically, while Jewish people were gathered in Jerusalem to celebrate the Old Covenant of the law, God was about to initiate an important part of his New Covenant in the Spirit.

14. Describe what happens in Acts 2:1-4 using descriptions of what the gathered 120 disciples would have experienced with their senses (touch, sight, hearing). What emotions do you think would have come along with these senses?

15. Notice that the tongues of fire rest on individuals. The New Testament later explains that the Holy Spirit indwells each believer individually. Look up these references and summarize their truth.

Romans 8:9-10

1 Corinthians 12:13

Galatians 4:6-7

Ephesians 1:13-14

16. What happens next in Acts 2:5-13? What are the gathered sojourners' reactions?

17. How do you think this miracle of languages affected the hearers later? Check the maps in your Bible to find these travelers' countries of origin. Why is it significant that people from a wide geographic area with different cultural backgrounds were gathered? Who is the gospel meant to reach (John 3:16)?

## Empowered

18. Don't miss the miracle in Acts 2:14. What does Peter do here? Recall Peter's actions fifty days earlier from Matthew 26:69-75. What has changed?

19. In Acts 2:17-21 Peter recalls Joel's prophecy. What is Peter telling the crowd about the sensory miracle they have seen?

20. The next thing Peter does is exactly what Jesus commissioned him to do in Acts 1:8. What is one main purpose of the power of the Holy Spirit?

21. As we move forward in future lessons, we will ponder the fact that the Holy Spirit indwells us as believers and produces the spiritual fruit of obedience to his commandments and deep character change. However, we must not miss the importance of the Holy Spirit's power for witnessing about Jesus. Read the rest of Peter's speech in Acts 2:22-36 and make a list of everything he teaches the crowd about Jesus.

22. We may not have opportunities to deliver speeches to mass audiences, but we have many opportunities to talk about Jesus. How can you make talking about Jesus a natural part of your conversations? How might you know when someone is open to talking about Jesus? How do you know when the Holy Spirit is leading you to speak?

23. One of the ways we can discern that someone is open to hearing about Jesus is by noticing what kinds of questions they ask. Open people ask honest questions; closed people often want to attack. We are to witness to both kinds of people. From Colossians 4:3-6 and 1 Peter 3:14-16, what demeanor do we use when we tell others about Jesus? Why does our demeanor matter?

24. One way to prepare to give a defense for the hope you have is by preparing a two-minute version of your story of coming to faith. Write that story here:

25. Another way to prepare to share about Jesus is to know a simple explanation of the salvation message from memory. Write out the main points of the salvation message here and include scriptures to support your points. (If you are stumped, use Peter's speech as a guide or google the "Romans Road" to salvation or the "Bridge Illustration" of salvation.)

## A Good Question

26. Let's head back to the Acts 2 narrative. What great question does the crowd ask Peter in Acts 2:37-38? What motivates the question? What part did the Holy Spirit play in their question? (Remember John 16:8-9.)

27. How does Peter answer the question in Acts 2:38-40? List each truth separately.

28. Why is each part of Peter's gospel invitation critical for his hearers? What happens if parts of this invitation are missing?

29. What were the results of Peter's first sermon in Acts 2:41?

30. Evaluate Jesus' promise from Acts 1:8 based on the events of Acts 2. What important power will the Holy Spirit have in every generation?

31. To end your study, write a prayer asking the Lord to make you sensitive to the Holy Spirit and empowered by him so that you can witness about Jesus.

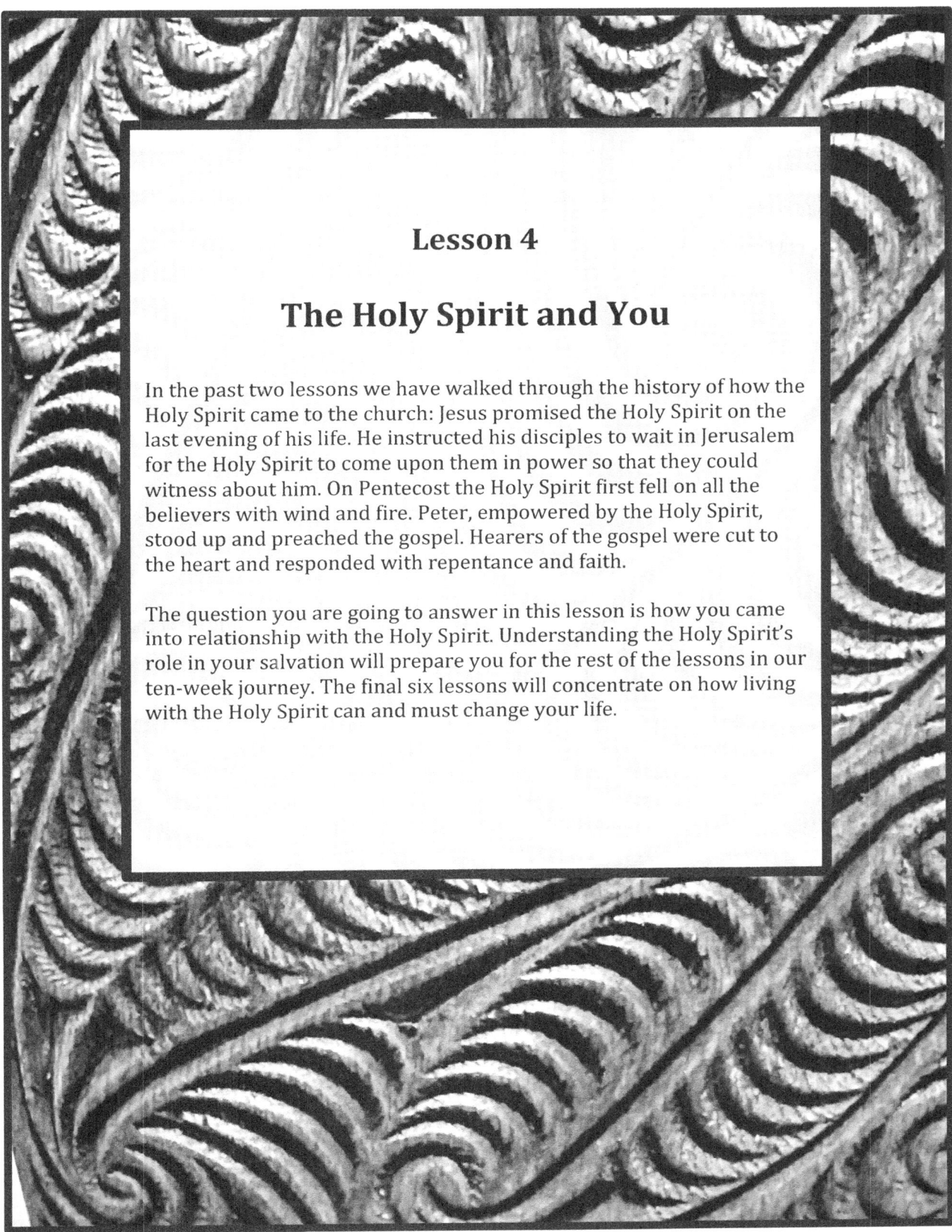

# Lesson 4

# The Holy Spirit and You

In the past two lessons we have walked through the history of how the Holy Spirit came to the church: Jesus promised the Holy Spirit on the last evening of his life. He instructed his disciples to wait in Jerusalem for the Holy Spirit to come upon them in power so that they could witness about him. On Pentecost the Holy Spirit first fell on all the believers with wind and fire. Peter, empowered by the Holy Spirit, stood up and preached the gospel. Hearers of the gospel were cut to the heart and responded with repentance and faith.

The question you are going to answer in this lesson is how you came into relationship with the Holy Spirit. Understanding the Holy Spirit's role in your salvation will prepare you for the rest of the lessons in our ten-week journey. The final six lessons will concentrate on how living with the Holy Spirit can and must change your life.

## *Daily Exercise Three*: Witness

In last week's lesson we learned about the coming of the Holy Spirit at Pentecost. We saw how the Holy Spirit enabled Peter to witness with power and effectiveness. In 2 Corinthians 3:4-6 Paul makes it clear that no one is sufficient to bring the gospel on their own. Our sufficiency comes only through the Spirit who gives life and brings freedom (2 Corinthians 3:17).

As a part of last week's lesson, you wrote your story of coming to faith in Jesus and also a brief explanation of the gospel. Both of these are crucial to witnessing about Jesus, but they are the last steps in witnessing. In this exercise, you will practice two of the first steps: prayer and relationship building. For this week, commit to daily prayer for three people that you know who don't yet believe in Jesus. Choose three people to pray for by name.

1.

2.

3.

- Pray that the Holy Spirit would bring spiritual desire to them.
- Pray the veil that blinds them to the gospel would be lifted. (2 Corinthians 3:15-16).
- Pray that they would come face to face with their sin and feel godly grief that leads to repentance (2 Corinthians 7:10).
- Pray for an opportunity for a gospel conversation (Colossians 4:3-4).

In addition, consider honing the skill of asking questions and listening to answers, then asking more follow-up questions. This shows you are truly listening and seeking to understand, learning to express genuine curiosity about other people's lives and thoughts. Honing your question asking skills will help you build relationships. Try some of these questions with believers to start. Then if an opportunity arises with an unbeliever, or even with one of the people you are praying for, you will be more comfortable asking.

Some open-ended questions that may lead to deeper conversation:
- I noticed _____, and I am curious. Can you tell me more about that?
- That's an interesting thought. Can you tell me more about how you came to believe that?
- What other options or evidence did you consider before you came to that opinion?
- What do you think has shaped you as a person, for better and for worse?
- How are you planning for your future?
- What part of your life do you really enjoy; what frustrates you?

If you are interested in becoming a more effective witness, you may want to read *God Space: Naturally Creating Room for Spiritual Conversations* by Doug Pollock.

## You Were Dead

1. This is a bleak place to start our lesson, but spiritual death is the real condition of every human born since Adam. If we don't reckon with spiritual death, we will never hunger for spiritual life. Read these scriptures and describe spiritual death.

John 3:18-19

Romans 3:10-12

Romans 5:12

Romans 8:6-8

Ephesians 2:1-3

2. Did you sense spiritual deadness before putting your faith in Jesus? Why or why not?

3. One initial experience with the Holy Spirit comes in relationship to our sin and spiritual deadness. What does Jesus say the Holy Spirit will do in John 16:8? How did you experience conviction over your sin?

4.  The gospel as found in the Scriptures—whether read, preached, shared in conversation, or taught—is critical for true repentance that leads to salvation. No one comes to salvation without knowledge of Jesus. Use these passages to describe the Scripture's or Holy Spirit's role in the gospel call to repentance.

Romans 10:13-17

1 Corinthians 2:1-5

2 Corinthians 3:4-6

1 Thessalonians 1:5

5.  Who shared the gospel with you? Did you believe quickly, or did you have several people share it with you? The Holy Spirit was at work in that person or people! (You may consider writing this person or people a note to thank them for sharing the gospel with you.)

## Internal Call of the Holy Spirit

The Holy Spirit works in the person sharing the gospel and he also works in the one who receives the gospel. In our last lesson we concentrated on how the Holy Spirit empowers believers to witness—as he did in Peter's case. Now, let's look at how the Holy Spirit helps a person—who is dead in their sin—to respond in faith. The theological term for this work is regeneration. Regeneration is when the Holy Spirit interacts with a spiritually dead person to make them alive to the gospel so that they will respond with faith. True regeneration is always coupled with saving faith.

6. Jesus taught about the regeneration of the Holy Spirit in a conversation early in his ministry. A religious leader named Nicodemus came to Jesus under cover of night to ask him questions. What Jesus said surprised and mystified him. Read John 3:1-8 and begin to explain what the Holy Spirit does to enable a person to enter the kingdom of heaven.

7. The Holy Spirit is the initiator of spiritual rebirth or regeneration. He moves like the wind in unseen ways, but with real effects. Regeneration is also described in Titus 3:5-7. What descriptions are used for regeneration in Titus 3:5? What does each of these teach us about the Holy Spirit's action?

8. Consider Ezekiel's prophecy in Ezekiel 36:25-27 along with 1 Corinthians 6:9-11. What kind of change does the Spirit bring?

9. True regeneration is always paired with the human response of genuine faith in the saving work of Jesus through his death and resurrection. Use these verses to describe the important role of faith in salvation.

John 1:12

John 3:16-18

Romans 10:8-13

Ephesians 2:4-9

10. Scripture contrasts salvation by faith with salvation by works or by the law. Can a person be saved by following the Old Testament laws or by good works? Use Romans 3:20-26 and Ephesians 2:9-10 to explain. How does this also confirm the Holy Spirit's role in salvation?

11. Think about how you came to faith in Jesus. Were you aware that God was drawing you to faith through his Spirit at the time? If so, how? If not, how would you describe God's action through the Spirit as you look back at what he did at that time of your life?

## Spiritual Adoption

12. The Holy Spirit worked—before you believed—to open your eyes to the gospel. He worked to cause you to be reborn by grace, through faith. He also continually bears witness in your heart that God has permanently adopted you as his child. Read Romans 8:14-16 and Galatians 4:4-7. How does salvation change your relationship with God? How does the Holy Spirit use your emotions to confirm your new relationship with God? (See also Romans 5:5.)

13. What does it mean to you that you are now a son or daughter of God? How could this change the way you interact with him in prayer and worship?

14. Believers are true children of God, and the Holy Spirit bears witness in our hearts that this is so. Nevertheless, this witness is not meant to be merely an emotional confirmation that we belong to God as Father. What lifestyle response does our status as God's child demand? Consider Ephesians 5:1-8 and 1 Peter 1:14-18.

## Seal and Pledge

We will spend the final six lessons of this study thinking through what it means for our daily life that the Spirit is with us and in us. We have much to learn about being filled with the Spirit, walking in the Spirit, bearing the fruit of the Holy Spirit, and using the gifts of the Holy Spirit. To end our study on how we came into relationship with the Holy Spirit, we must consider the truth that the Holy Spirit indwells us and is given to us as a seal and a pledge.

15. Once a person has been united with Christ through the regeneration of the Holy Spirit and faith, that person is indwelt by the Holy Spirit permanently. Use these passages to confirm that the Holy Spirit lives inside a believer. What does the Holy Spirit give as he indwells a believer? What is a believer's response to this indwelling?

Romans 8:9-11

1 Corinthians 3:16; 6:19-20

2 Timothy 1:13-14

16. In Ephesians 1:3-14 Paul describes our heavenly inheritance. You'll notice our adoption as sons in verse 5. According to verse 11, we obtain our inheritance as a result of our sonship. Use 1 Peter 1:3-5 to describe this inheritance.

17. In Ephesians 1:13 it says believers are sealed with the Holy Spirit. The Greek word for sealed is *sphragizo*. It means to seal in the same way a letter is sealed with a wax stamp. This kind of stamp keeps the correspondence secure and unmistakably marks it as coming from the sender. What does this image say about the Holy Spirit's role in our salvation?

18. In Ephesians 1:14 it describes the Holy Spirit as a guarantee or pledge of our inheritance. The Greek word *arrabon* means a down payment or deposit given in good faith that the remaining payment would certainly come in the future. What is the certain future of believers? (Consider 1 Corinthians 15:50-57 and 2 Corinthians 5:1-5.)

19. Finish your study by considering how the Holy Spirit convicted you of sin, called you to repentance, caused you to be born again by grace through faith, confirmed your adoption as a son or daughter, and has sealed you for the day that you will be glorified in heaven. Write a prayer of worship and response to this truth.

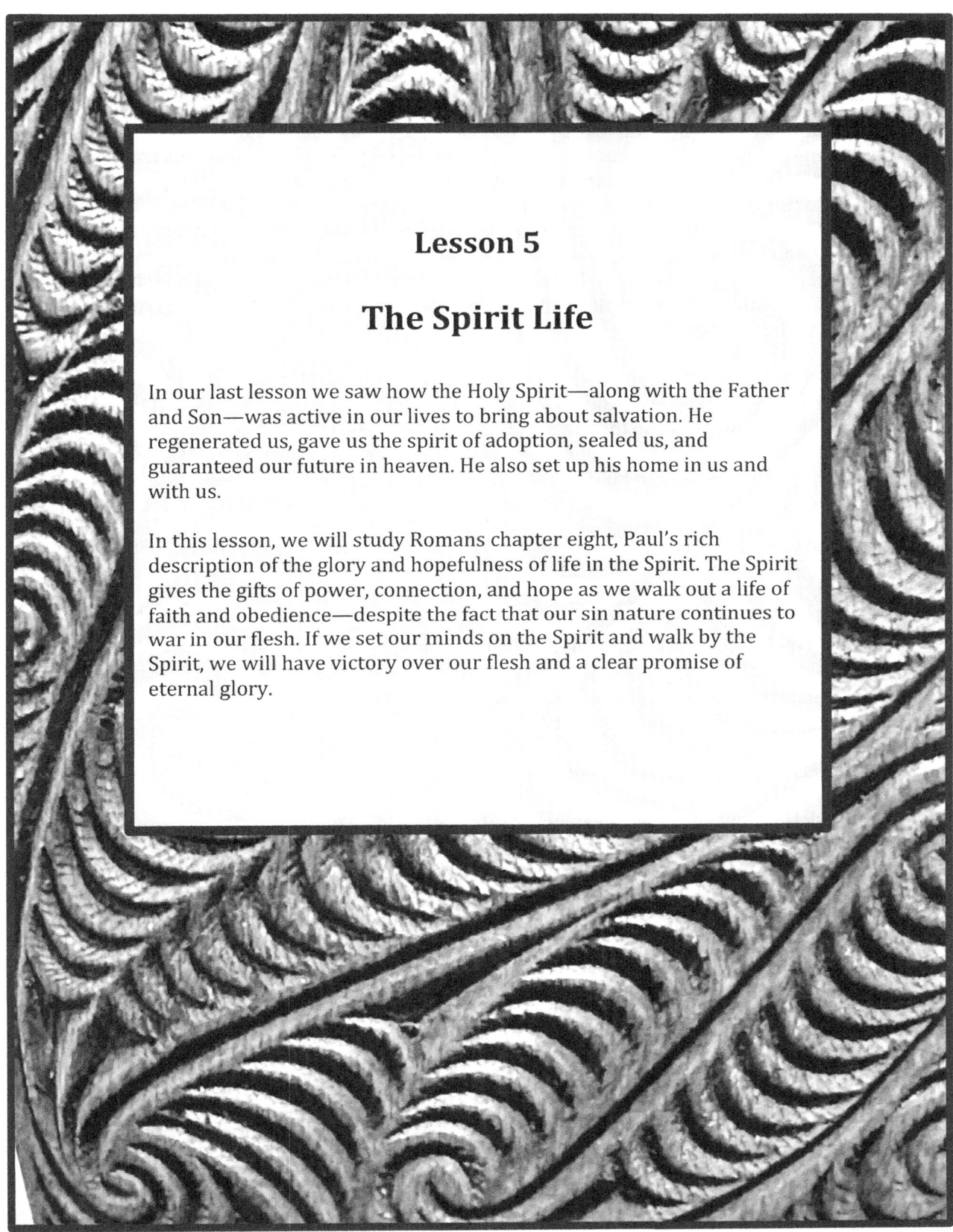

# Lesson 5

# The Spirit Life

In our last lesson we saw how the Holy Spirit—along with the Father and Son—was active in our lives to bring about salvation. He regenerated us, gave us the spirit of adoption, sealed us, and guaranteed our future in heaven. He also set up his home in us and with us.

In this lesson, we will study Romans chapter eight, Paul's rich description of the glory and hopefulness of life in the Spirit. The Spirit gives the gifts of power, connection, and hope as we walk out a life of faith and obedience—despite the fact that our sin nature continues to war in our flesh. If we set our minds on the Spirit and walk by the Spirit, we will have victory over our flesh and a clear promise of eternal glory.

## *Daily Exercise Four*: **Filling**

In Ephesians chapter four, Paul teaches about laying aside the old way of life and living a renewed life in Christ. He commands us to be renewed in the spirit of our minds and then put off our old life and put on a new life. This put off/put on cycle happens according to the Spirit of renewal. In this context, he tells us in Ephesians 4:30 not to grieve the Holy Spirit. The Spirit of God actually grieves—has a painful emotional reaction—when we fail to live this new kind of life. Then, in Ephesians 5:15-20, Paul continues to tell us how to walk in love, having put away former behaviors of disobedience. In Ephesians 5:18 we find the core idea of this section. It tells us to be filled with the Holy Spirit. Disobedience grieves the Holy Spirit; filling by the Holy Spirit moves us to the obedient life.

Every believer has the Holy Spirit. He or she is permanently indwelt, sealed, and adopted. Every believer is not, however automatically filled with the Holy Spirit. To be filled with the Spirit means to be controlled by the influence of the Spirit. In Ephesians 5:18 it commands that a believer not let wine have control, but instead be filled with the Spirit. This is an apt contrast because it gives us the idea of being under the influence. Just as wine creates a state of drunkenness, the Holy Spirit creates the state of thankful, worshipful, obedience in us.

After commanding us to be filled with the Spirit in Ephesians 5:18, it describes the results of being filled with the Spirit.
- We speak to one another with Psalms, hymns, and spiritual songs. (We encourage one another with worshipful, spiritual truth.)
- We make melody in our hearts to God with singing. (We have a heart bent toward worship.)
- We give thanks in everything to God.
- We submit to one another, putting others first.

Your exercise for each day of this week is threefold.

1. Ask the Holy Spirit to fill you with gratefulness. Each day thank the Lord for at least five new things. Do this in a spirit of worship and prayer, but you may want to write them down as well.

2. Pray each morning that the Holy Spirit will give you an opportunity to share an encouraging word to another believer. Keep your eyes open for the opportunities the Holy Spirit brings.

3. Ask the Holy Spirit to reveal to you any behaviors that grieve him. Truly embrace any conviction the Holy Spirit sends your way. Agree with him in confession and ask for forgiveness. This conviction is an invitation to deeper obedience and intimacy with God. As he brings something to mind, think of a way you could take steps to put that behavior off and put on the godly alternative. Then ask for the Holy Spirit's filling influence to move in the direction of obedience.

## The Battle

1. Paul writes the first six chapters of Romans explaining the problem of sin. He presents Jesus' atoning sacrifice as the provision for the forgiveness of sin—by grace through faith. In chapter seven his tone changes and becomes more personal. He expresses the personal frustration of living with a sinful nature—even after being saved, forgiven, and freed from the penalty of sin. In Romans 7:15-24 his frustration reaches its climax. Read Romans 7:15-24 and summarize Paul's frustration. What problem does he face? What emotion does he feel?

2. Define "the flesh" based on Romans 7:18. (You may want to use a Greek expository dictionary or your study Bible's notes.)

3. Every believer does battle with their sin nature. As you read Paul's account of his frustration with sin, what came to mind for you? What repeatedly tempts you? What do you do that you don't want to do? What do you desire to do that you don't do? Be honest, because as this lesson continues you will be using these areas of your life as an opportunity for application.

## No Condemnation

4. The very real battle a believer faces with sin could lead to perpetual frustration without the truth that Paul shares next. Start by defining condemnation as used in Romans 8:1.

5. According to Romans 8:1-3 why is there no more condemnation for sin for those who are in Christ Jesus? Who paid the price of condemnation and how did he do it? (Also see Romans 5:16-18.)

6. What does the Spirit offer in place of condemnation according to Romans 8:2? What do these things mean?

7. How does the offer of life and freedom change the way you view your ongoing battle with sin? How does the secure knowledge that, if you are in Christ Jesus, you won't face eternal condemnation change the way you approach your battle with sin?

8. From Romans 8:4 what is the goal of our lives as believers? How do we live out this goal?

## The Mind

9. A life in the Spirit relies at least partly on what we do with our minds. Read Romans 8:5-8 and describe the person who sets their mind on the flesh. What is the result of a mind set on the flesh?

10. Paul's language suggests that a believer's life is not marked by the pattern of setting his or her mind on the flesh—that pattern marks life of an unbeliever. Yet if we are honest—as Paul was in chapter seven—we know that we can slide into fleshly thinking. If a believer sets his or her mind on the flesh, what will this look like in daily life? What would be his or her focus and priority?

11. According to Romans 8:5-6 what does it mean to set your mind on the Spirit? What are the results of setting your mind on the Spirit? How do your priorities change?

12. What daily practices would show that you are setting your mind on the Spirit? Describe your experience of the Spirit when you do these things.

13. Think again about the struggle you named earlier in the lesson. How could setting your mind on the Spirit change this struggle? How could you change your thinking about this struggle? How would setting your mind on the Spirit change the way you find strength for this battle?

## The Spirit in You

14. In Romans 8:9 it proclaims that the Holy Spirit's indwelling presence is the fundamental difference between the person who has Christ and the person who doesn't. What does it mean in verse 10 when it says that the body is dead because of sin, yet the Spirit is life because of righteousness? (See Romans 3:21-26.)

15. How does Romans 8:11 describe the Holy Spirit? What can the Spirit do in you? When will the Spirit do this?

16. According to Romans 8:12-13 we don't owe anything to the flesh. In fact, if we live according to the flesh we will die. Instead, what is our aim according to Romans 8:13?

17. What does this mean as you think of your particular struggle against sin? How can you put to death the deeds of the body? (Some ideas to consider: Consult the Word about this area of struggle; pray about ways to be kept from this temptation; or replace this sin with the opposite virtue.)

## Spirit of Sonship

18. In Romans 8:14-16 we are reminded again of the special relationship that the Holy Spirit creates for us. Who are we according to this passage?

19. What contrast does Romans 8:15 present? How is the spirit of slavery different than the spirit of sonship?

20. How do you feel about your status as son or daughter of God? How does it motivate and affirm you? How does this relationship help you to put sin to death?

21. Consider both your battle against sin and the idea of a totally renewed fearless life in the Spirit. How could your relationship with the Holy Spirit renew, empower, and guide you? Are there any areas of your life that you have closed off to the Spirit's power? How can you open yourself fully to the Holy Spirit?

22. Write a prayer asking for resurrection power to live by the Spirit as you put to death the deeds of the flesh and live an abundant Spirit-led life.

# Lesson 6

# Glory and Groaning

As we continue in Romans eight, we recall that the Spirit confirms in our spirits that we have been adopted by the Father as sons and daughters. One of the results of becoming sons and daughters is that we are also his heirs. We can be sure of this inheritance and rely on the Spirit to bring our faith to completion by one day glorifying our bodies and souls in heaven. In the meantime, however, we groan along with all creation waiting for this to happen.

As we wait, the Spirit searches our spirits. He helps us to pray according to the Father's will and intercedes for us. This intercession and life in the Spirit make all the difference as we walk the road of groaning on the way to glory. Romans eight goes on to remind us that all things work together for good for those who love God. He is at work to conform us to the image of the Son. Therefore, God's love, through Christ, in the power of the Holy Spirit makes us more than conquerors.

## *Daily Exercise Five*: Examine

As we've considered the action of the Holy Spirit, we haven't spent much time in the Old Testament, but it also contains important truth. In Psalm 139:1-12 it describes God's omniscience and his omnipresence. God knows everything about us: every thought, motive, and action. In Psalm 139:7 it asks the questions, "Where shall I go from your Spirit? Or where shall I flee from your presence?" It goes on the answer that God is everywhere. This reassuring truth is similar to Jesus' promise to never leave us nor forsake us, and to send the Helper. However, near the end of the Psalm, David comes to another conclusion. If God knows everything, then we can ask him to search our hearts to see if there is any grievous way in us. We can ask him to guide us into the "everlasting way."

In the first three chapters of Revelation, Jesus appears to John in a Spirit-led vision. In this vision, Jesus gives John messages for seven first-century churches. In these messages, it is clear that Jesus sees and knows everything about these churches. In some areas, he is pleased with what he sees, but in others he has charges against them. He has seen their actions and motives clearly and is not pleased. At the end of each warning he says, "He who has an ear, let him hear what the Spirit says to the churches." We can assume that Jesus sees us in the same way. We would do well to ask Jesus for his true estimation of our lives and give ear to the Spirit as he examines our actions and motives.

Last week your exercise was about asking for filling of the Holy Spirit as you set your mind on thankfulness, encouraging others, and changing any areas of disobedience. This week you are going to continue in those same practices in the morning.

In the evening, before you go to bed, add a time of heart examination.

- Before you go to bed each evening this week, talk over your day with God. Ask the Holy Spirit to help you remember your day. Did you ask for filling? Did you look for opportunities to act out of his filling?

- Likely, there will be some memories that are really encouraging. Celebrate these with worship and thanksgiving.

- Probably there will be some missed opportunities or failures. If the Spirit brings any of these to mind, confess them and ask for forgiveness.

- Reaffirm your desire to be filled with the Holy Spirit.

- Sleep soundly in his care.

## Future Glory

1. In Romans 8:16-17 what does the Spirit reveal to the believer's spirit about being a child and an heir? What condition does he include?

2. In Romans 8:18 what comparison is offered? How does this shed light on the goodness of our glorious inheritance?

3. In 1 Peter 1:3-5 it also describes this glorious inheritance. How does this passage describe our inheritance?

4.  Describe the glory of heaven as revealed in Revelation 21:1-7.

5.  How does the sure promise of glorification in heaven with God change the way you view difficulty, your battle with sin, or suffering?

## Groaning

6.  In Romans 8:19-22 what groans and why does it groan? Where did this suffering come from? (See Genesis 3:16-19.) How does the brokenness of creation affect humanity?

7. Who suffers or groans according to Romans 8:23? What does it mean to have first fruits of the Holy Spirit in the context of what we have learned about life in the Spirit in Romans eight so far?

8. What do groaning believers long for according to Romans 8:23-24? What does it mean to hope and have patience in this waiting?

9. Some of the effects of living in a fallen creation are living with disease, natural disasters, and difficulty in work and in relationships. How do you respond when you have to suffer these effects of living in a fallen creation? What part do patience and hope have for you as you suffer? How can you grow in patience and hope while looking forward to the final glory of heaven?

## The Spirit Intercedes

10. Creation groans for the glorious time when the sons of God will be fully set free from the bondage of sin. Believers groan for this day as well. In Romans 8:26-27 it tells us that the Spirit groans in a different way. What does the Spirit do to help us in our suffering? What problem does he help us with? How does he help?

11. How might this change the way you pray when you are speechless or frustrated?

12. The Spirit's intercession is always according to the will of God. What is the result of the Spirit's intercession on our behalf according to Romans 8:28? Think about this thoroughly: What are "all" things? What does "our good" mean?

13. In Romans 8:29 Paul reminds us of God's will in calling us. What does Romans 8:29 say God calls believers to?

14. The Spirit is interceding for us so that we will be conformed to the image of the Son. What does it mean to be conformed to the image of the Son in *life*? (See Luke 9:23-24; Ephesians 4:17-24.)

15. What does it mean to be conformed to the image of the Son in *death*? (See 1 Corinthians 15:42-49.)

16. In Romans 8:29 it tells us it was God's will that Jesus be the firstborn among many brothers. What is God's action in salvation according to Romans 8:30? What is the progression of salvation? (Remember what you learned in Lesson 4 as well.)

## What Then

When we began studying the eighth chapter of Romans in our last lesson, Paul is responding to the frustration of having to live with an ongoing sin nature. In Romans eight he reminds himself and his readers that there is no condemnation in Christ Jesus and that the Spirit sets them free from sin and death. The mind set on the Spirit gives life. The Spirit confirms in our spirits that we are children of God. The Spirit reminds us that we are heirs of future glory. The Spirit intercedes for us according to the Father's will so that all things work together for good for us. Now Paul wraps up this whole section with his conclusions about the love of God. In context, we could also connect this love of God with the gift of the Holy Spirit. Remember how Jesus told his disciples that it would be better if he left so that the Spirit could come? Romans eight helps us appreciate this all the more.

17. In Romans 8:31-35 Paul asks a series of rhetorical questions. For each of these questions give an answer and consider the implications of that answer. How can you change the way you think about life? How can you change your actions? What part does the Holy Spirit play in these changes?

If God is for us who can be against us?

He who did not spare his own Son but gave him up for us all, how will he not also with him graciously give us all things?

Who shall bring any charge against God's elect?

It is God who justifies. Who is to condemn?

Christ is the one who died—more than that, who was raised—who is at the right hand of God, who indeed is interceding for us. Who shall separate us from the love of Christ?

Shall tribulation, or distress, or persecution, or famine, or nakedness, or danger, or sword?

18. In Romans 8:37-38 what conclusions does Paul draw about God's love? What assurance and power does this give you to live?

19. Think about a challenge in one of your relationships, difficult circumstances, or an opportunity that has come your way recently. How can God's love and the help of the Holy Spirit make you more than a conqueror?

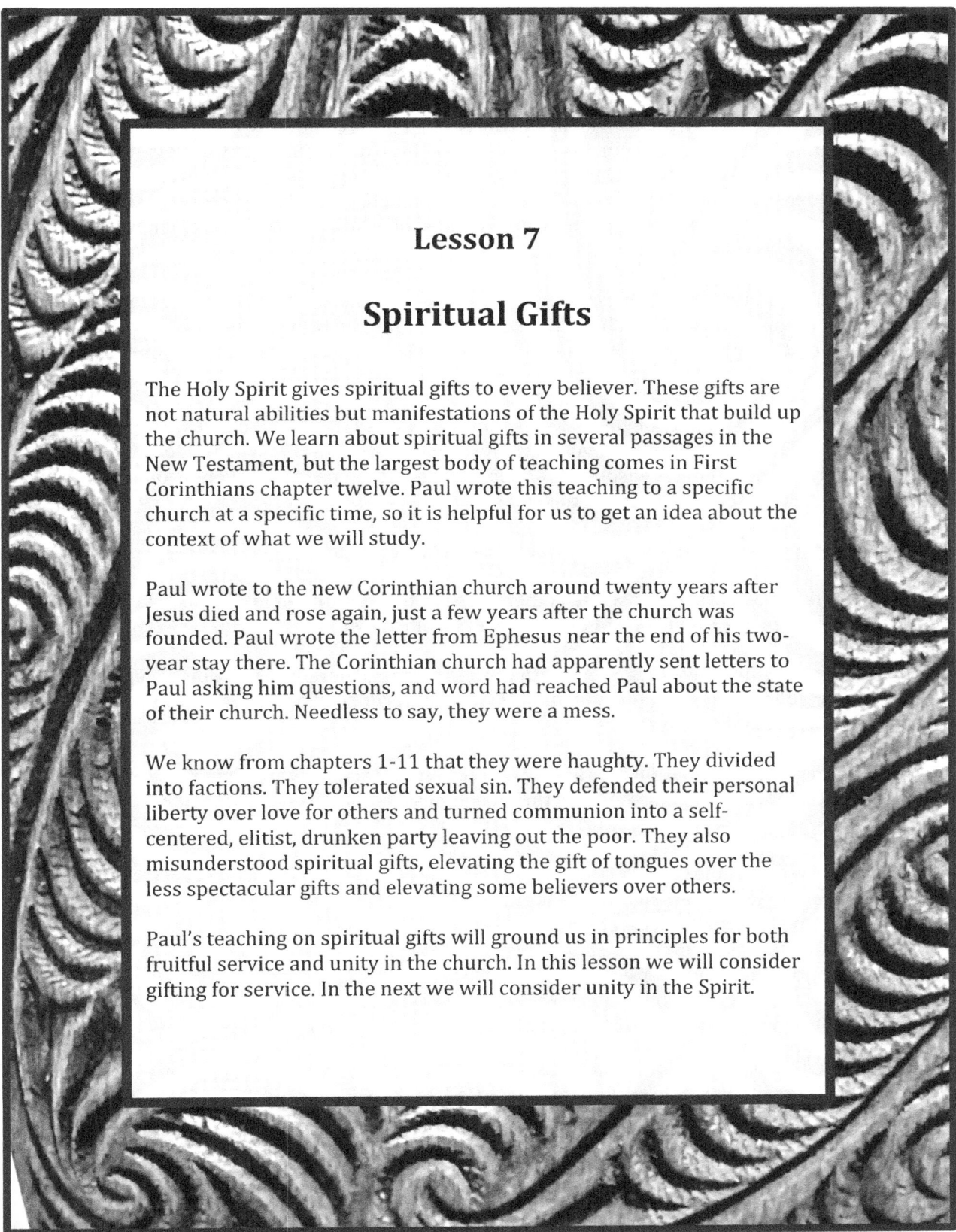

# Lesson 7

# Spiritual Gifts

The Holy Spirit gives spiritual gifts to every believer. These gifts are not natural abilities but manifestations of the Holy Spirit that build up the church. We learn about spiritual gifts in several passages in the New Testament, but the largest body of teaching comes in First Corinthians chapter twelve. Paul wrote this teaching to a specific church at a specific time, so it is helpful for us to get an idea about the context of what we will study.

Paul wrote to the new Corinthian church around twenty years after Jesus died and rose again, just a few years after the church was founded. Paul wrote the letter from Ephesus near the end of his two-year stay there. The Corinthian church had apparently sent letters to Paul asking him questions, and word had reached Paul about the state of their church. Needless to say, they were a mess.

We know from chapters 1-11 that they were haughty. They divided into factions. They tolerated sexual sin. They defended their personal liberty over love for others and turned communion into a self-centered, elitist, drunken party leaving out the poor. They also misunderstood spiritual gifts, elevating the gift of tongues over the less spectacular gifts and elevating some believers over others.

Paul's teaching on spiritual gifts will ground us in principles for both fruitful service and unity in the church. In this lesson we will consider gifting for service. In the next we will consider unity in the Spirit.

## *Daily Exercise Six*: **Wisdom**

The Holy Spirit is our helper as we live the Christian life. Much of what we need to know is plain in Scripture and the Holy Spirit helps us remember these things and gives us power to live them out as we put off the old life and put on the new. There are areas of life, however, that the Scripture doesn't explicitly address. There is no command about what career you should pursue, or where you should live. There are not specific instructions for many choices in life. These choices require wisdom.

Consider Paul's prayers in Ephesians 1:15-22 and Colossians 1:9-14. Both of these prayers ask for growing spiritual wisdom. Though they don't mention the Holy Spirit, we can't help but remember 1 Corinthians 2:11-16 where Paul says that wisdom and the mind of Christ come through the Spirit.

In James 1:5 it says, "If any of you lacks wisdom, let him ask of God, who gives generously to all without reproach, and it will be given him." Also consider James 3:17 where it describes the wisdom from God: "But the wisdom of God is first pure, then peaceable, gentle, open to reason, full of mercy and good fruits, impartial and sincere."

What decisions or situations are you facing that require wisdom?

Each day this week pray and ask the Father to speak to you through his Spirit. Ask him for wisdom. (Consider praying one of Paul's prayers from above.)

Know that the Spirit never disagrees with the Scriptures. (Therefore, you don't ever need to ask the Lord if you should cheat on your spouse, or hold a grudge in bitterness, for example. Scripture commands that you must not.)

As you process your situation in prayer and consider any actions you might take (or attitudes you might adopt), filter your thoughts through James 3:17 and its definition of wisdom.

Is this option pure?
Is this action peaceable?
Am I exercising gentleness in this situation?
Am I open to reason from wise believers?
Do my actions reflect mercy?
Will this option help me bear good fruit?
Would I be displaying ungodly favoritism with this option?
Do I sincerely want to please the Lord and act in wisdom, or do I just want my own way?

Be patient. God is not on your timetable. With all this in mind, you can confidently move forward if you are sincerely seeking to please God. Make a choice and serve God faithfully in that choice.

## One Spirit

1. In 1 Corinthians 12:4-6 Paul introduces spiritual gifts with the ideas that they are varied in some ways, but also the same. Read this passage in at least two translations. What is varied? What do each of these things mean? What point is he making by saying gifts and opportunities to use the gifts are varied?

2. In 1 Corinthians 12:4-6 what is the same? What is he saying about God? What is he saying about the gifts?

3. According to 1 Corinthians 12:6-7 why does the triune God give gifts? Add the wisdom of Ephesians 4:11-16 to your answer.

4. How does knowing the purpose of gifts change the way you view the gifts?

5. If God is the driving force behind the gifts, he decides how and when they are used. The gifts come from him for his purposes. What happens when a person uses a supposed gift for their own purposes and agenda?

## Many Gifts

6. The Greek word *charisma* is translated into the English word gift in this passage. It means a gift of grace or an undeserved benefit. How does this definition help you to view any gifts you receive rightly?

# Definitions

Defining the gifts is surprisingly difficult. The Greek words leave room for interpretation, and Paul himself does not describe them fully. If you read several commentaries, you will find an array of definitions. Often, these definitions seem to reflect the commentator's theological or denominational bent. As we attempt to define these gifts there is plenty of room for humility! The definitions below reflect my compiled understanding of the scholars I read. (See the bibliography.) You'll notice that each definition includes the Holy Spirit. I'm repeating this pre-supposition because it is crucial to our understanding of the gifts. The Holy Spirit is the initiator and empowering person behind these gifts. They are not natural abilities, but supernatural manifestations of the Holy Spirit's activity in a believer's life. He is the determining and driving force; we walk in step with him. We learn to use his gifts. We seek him and his gifts, but we are not ultimately an authority over the gift. These definitions include the gifts mentioned in 1 Corinthians 12:8-11, 28-31; Romans 12:6-8; and Ephesians 4:11.

**Utterance of Wisdom:** A Spirit-guided ability to speak spiritual wisdom (as opposed to natural or worldly) to another person. It could also mean the Spirit-guided ability to apply spiritual knowledge in a specific practical way.
Scripture: 1 Corinthians 12:8; 1 Corinthians 2:12-13

**Utterance of Knowledge:** The ability to speak information or knowledge (especially of God) that the Spirit brings to mind. It may be previously learned information. (This is difficult to distinguish from utterance of wisdom and may be similar in meaning.)
Scripture: 1 Corinthians 12:8, 13:2,8, 14:6; Ephesians 1:7

**Faith:** The Spirit-guided ability to trust in the promises or supernatural work of God for a specific situation. (This is distinguished from saving faith, which every believer has.)
Scripture: 1 Corinthians 12:9; 13:2; Mark 11:23; Romans 12:3

**Gifts of Healings:** A Spirit-empowered ability to heal a physical infirmity or disease. (The plural sense in the Greek might mean that the Spirit gives this according to his will, on occasion, in various ways, not as a gift that a certain "healer" has permanently at his or her disposal.)[1,2]
Scripture: 1 Corinthians 12:9,28,30; Acts 14:8-10

**Workings of Miracles:** A Spirit-empowered ability to display God's power through works (in addition to healing) that would be impossible in the normal, natural world. (The plural sense may have the same implications as gifts of healings.)
Scripture: 1 Corinthians 12:10, 28-29; 2 Corinthians 12:12; Romans 15:19; Acts 6:8; Acts 8:5-8; Acts 19:11-15

**Prophecy:** A spontaneous, Spirit-guided revelation meant to be delivered verbally and intelligibly to other people, yet remain subject to testing, Scripture and group interpretation. Some suggest this is actually similar to preaching or proclaiming the truth of Scripture.
Scripture: 1 Corinthians 12:10, 13:2, 14:1,29-33, 11:4-5; Acts 2:16-18, 21:9; 1 Thessalonians 5:19-21

**Ability to Distinguish Between Spirits:** A Spirit-guided ability to tell the difference between the Spirit of God, the human spirit, and evil spirits or false teachers.
Scripture: 1 Corinthians 12:10; 14:29; 1 John 4:1

**Tongues:** The Spirit-given ability to speak to God in a language unknown to the speaker, unintelligible to other hearers except those with a gift of interpretation. This speech is simultaneously under the control of the Spirit and self-controlled by the speaker. (Meaning the speaker is not in a trance or some less than mindful state.)
Scripture: 1 Corinthians 12:10,30, 13:1.8, 14:2-33; Acts 2:2-8

**Interpretation of Tongues:** The Spirit-given ability to understand a tongue being spoken in public, either by the tongues speaker, or another person.
Scripture: 1 Corinthians 12:10, 30, 14:5,13,26-28

**Apostle:** This literally means "one sent on a mission." Jesus himself was called an apostle. (Hebrews 3:1) In most references, apostle refers to an office or role. Apostles were those who had seen Jesus and were leaders in the early church starting with the eleven disciples and Matthias in place of Judas. Christ himself appointed Paul apostle to the Gentiles. Other men of the early church were also called apostles or messengers. The office of apostle ceased with the death of those eyewitness apostles. The gift of one who advances the church may continue. Some would call them missionaries or church-planters.
Scripture: 1 Corinthians 12:28; Acts 1:2, 22-26; Ephesians 3:4-5, 4:11; 2 Corinthians 12:12

**Teacher:** The Spirit-empowered ability to teach others the things of God, especially Scripture.
Scripture: 1 Corinthians 12:28; Acts 13:1; Ephesians 4:11; 2 Timothy 1:11; James 3:1.

**Helping:** The Spirit-led ability to come alongside others to help them, especially as they minister to the needs of others.
Scripture: 1 Corinthians 12:28 (This Greek word is only found here in the New Testament.)

**Administration:** The Spirit-led ability to steer or guide others and create and execute effective plans. This is a leadership gift.
Scripture: 1 Corinthians 12:28 (This Greek word is only found here in the New Testament.)

**Giving:** The supernatural ability to share or contribute and be generous beyond the normal or expected.
Scripture: Romans 12:8, 2 Corinthians 8:1-3

**Mercy:** The Spirit-led ability to show compassion or kind concern
Scripture: Romans 12:8

**Exhortation:** The Spirit-led ability to help, comfort, or encourage with words.
Scripture: Romans 12:8; Acts 15:32; 1 Thessalonians 5:11

**Evangelist:** One who is gifted by the Spirit to share the gospel (good news) effectively.
Scripture: Ephesians 4:11; 2 Timothy 4:5

**Shepherd:** One who is given the Spirit-led ability to pastor or shepherd others caring for their spiritual well-being.
Scripture: Ephesians 4:11; John 21:15-17

---

[1] R. C. H. Lenski, *The Interpretation of St. Paul's First and Second Epistle to the Corinthians*, (Minneapolis, MN: Augsburg Publishing House, 1963), 501–502.
[2] Anthony C. Thiselton, *The First Epistle to the Corinthians: A Commentary on the Greek Text*, New International Greek Testament Commentary, (Grand Rapids, MI: W.B. Eerdmans, 2000), 948.

7.  As you read through the definitions of the gifts, do any stand out to you as gifts that you have sensed the Spirit empowering in your life since becoming a believer? (Remember these are not natural abilities, but supernatural giftings.) If so, how did you know it was from God? If not, why do you think you are not in touch with your spiritual gifts?

8.  How can you discern that the Spirit is giving you a gift? What part does the community of believers play in helping you discern how the Holy Spirit is gifting you?

9.  How can you discern when he is specifically empowering you to use your gifts in a situation? How would you seek his filling or empowering in a situation?

10. Give an example of a time when you used one of your spiritual gifts. What were the results of using this gift?

## Gifts in You

11. Read Romans 12:3-8. According to verses 3 and 6 what is the proper view of oneself in relationship to gifts?

12. What does Romans 12:6-8 say about the vigor with which we exercise gifts? Why does this matter?

13. What can you do to grow in your particular gifts? How can you rely more heavily on the Holy Spirit for this growth?

14. Look back at question three and the purposes of gifts. Now that you have considered your own gifts, how do you think your gifts fit in to help the body mature and build itself up in love? (Consider Ephesians 4:11-16 again.)

15. How do your gifts help equip or inspire others for the work of ministry? How do other people's gifts help inspire and equip you for the work of the ministry? Give some examples.

16. What affect do you think you have on the body as you exercise the gifts the Spirit gives you? What is your impact in your local church?

17. What would happen to your local church if you did not respond to the Holy Spirit and use your gifts? Why do you matter to your local body?

18. What action can you take this week to seek the Spirit and his gifts?

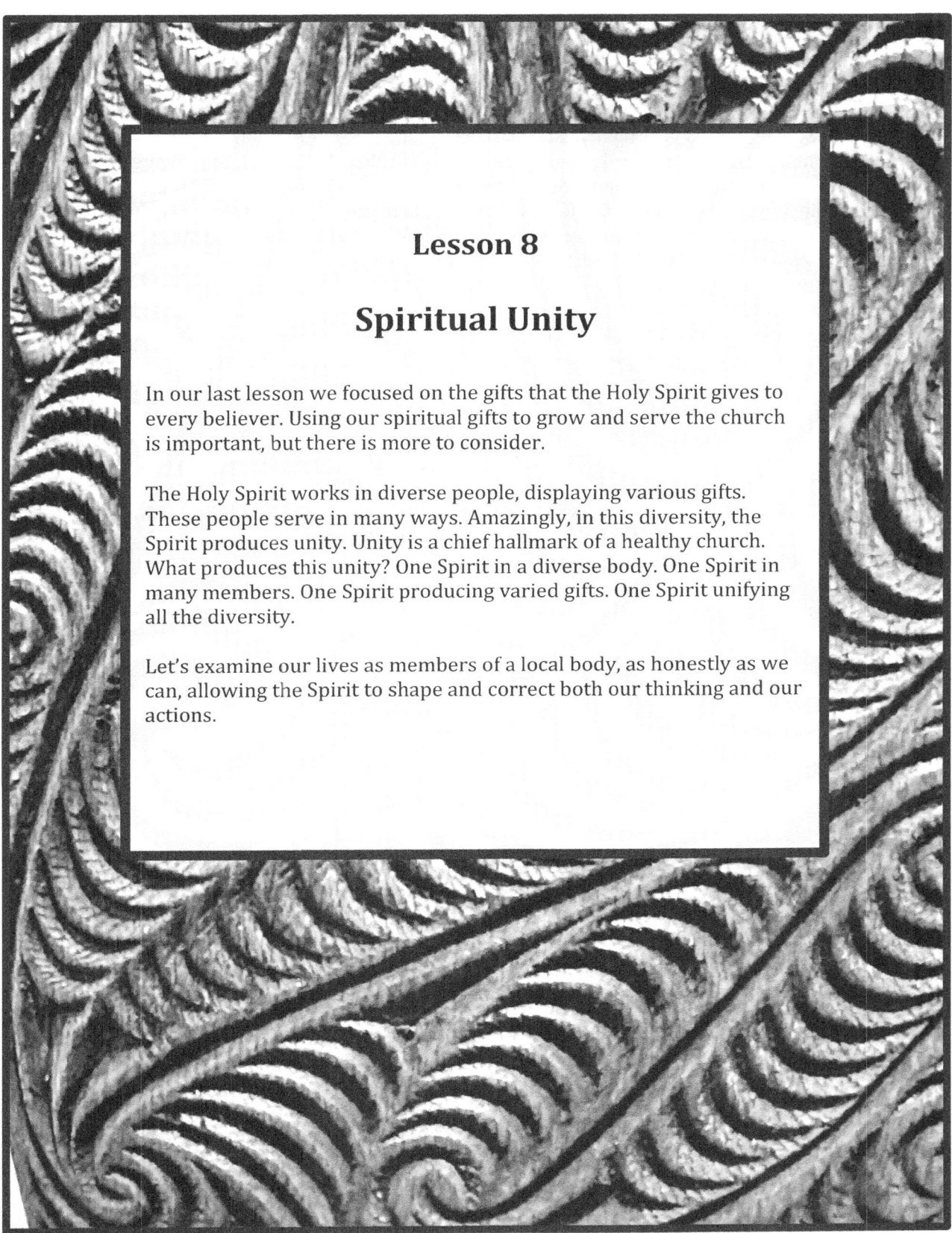

# Lesson 8

# Spiritual Unity

In our last lesson we focused on the gifts that the Holy Spirit gives to every believer. Using our spiritual gifts to grow and serve the church is important, but there is more to consider.

The Holy Spirit works in diverse people, displaying various gifts. These people serve in many ways. Amazingly, in this diversity, the Spirit produces unity. Unity is a chief hallmark of a healthy church. What produces this unity? One Spirit in a diverse body. One Spirit in many members. One Spirit producing varied gifts. One Spirit unifying all the diversity.

Let's examine our lives as members of a local body, as honestly as we can, allowing the Spirit to shape and correct both our thinking and our actions.

## *Daily Exercise Seven*: Service

The Holy Spirit gives us gifts specifically so that we will use them! In our last lesson we saw that there are many varieties of service and good work which the Holy Spirit empowers. In fact, they are as varied as people are varied. You will see in this week's lesson that every Christian plays a crucial role in the body of Christ. It follows that if you are not engaged in serving and using your gifts, both you and those around you are missing an important opportunity for growth and maturity. Ephesians 2:10 tells us that God has actually prepared good works for us so that we will walk in them.

Every day this week you will ask the Holy Spirit a few simple questions. Seek to listen for his answers. Purpose to be very aware of opportunities that the Spirit presents.

- Who can I serve today?
- Where would you like to use me today?
- Spirit, what opportunity will you give me today to use the gifts you have given?

In addition to praying these questions each day, use this week to prayerfully evaluate your ongoing service commitments. Consider some of these questions to help you evaluate your service. Jot down some thoughts this week.

What are my main spiritual gifts?


What service opportunities have I committed myself to:

Daily

Weekly

Monthly

As needs arise


How do these opportunities fit with my gifts and am I really seeking and relying on the Holy Spirit's power and guidance as I serve in these ways?


What changes might I make to better align my service and my giftedness?


How can I stretch to rely more fully on the power the Holy Spirit provides as I serve?

## Diverse Body

Read 1 Corinthians 12:12-27 to get the flow of thought in the whole passage we will study this week. You'll notice that Paul doesn't concentrate on an individual "finding his or her spiritual gifts." Instead, he focuses on how to view spiritual gifts in the context of life with others in the body of Christ. The big theme in this section is unity amid diversity.

1. In 1 Corinthians 12:12-13 what makes us one though we are many? When is a person baptized in the Spirit? (See Ephesians 1:13-14.)

2. We may think that variety is only found in the gifts and the ways they are used. However, 1 Corinthians 12:13 tells us that variety is also displayed in people's socio-economic background, nationality, religious background, and ethnicity. The world divides over these differences. How is the church supposed to think about these differences? Think of some benefits of unity amid diversity.

3. Philippians 2:1-4 gives us beautiful picture of what unity in diversity could look like. Go through this passage verse by verse and describe the behaviors of spiritual unity.

4. Read on in Philippians 2:5-8. What kind of mindset will you need to live out unity amid diversity? Why is humility so important?

5. What comes to mind in your life as you read Philippians 2:1-4? Evaluate your actions in your relationships with family and friends at church.

6. Evaluate your local church on its commitment to embracing and valuing all people. What is your church doing well? Where could it improve? What part do you play in this?

## View of Self

7.  In 1 Corinthians 12:14-16 Paul uses the analogy of the members of a body to illustrate an incorrect way of looking at gifts in the context of a church community. In this analogy, what are the foot and ear saying? What do they think of themselves? What conclusion do they draw when they compare?

8.  We are all prone to compare ourselves with others. What motivates comparison for you?

9.  What happens when you compare yourself to others? Have you had the experience of considering yourself unimportant? Why?

10. In 1 Corinthians 12:17-20 what is Paul saying to those who feel inferior to others? What does he want every person in the church to know? How does this affect your thinking about yourself? What is a healthy perspective on yourself?

11. If you hear someone in your church saying that they are unimportant, what can you do to help them? How can you affirm another person's giftedness? Why is this important?

12. Think about your service in your local body. What injury to the body would be created if you stopped serving? If you don't serve, what is holding you back? How could you reprioritize to play your vital role in the body?

## Independence vs. Interdependence

13. In 1 Corinthians 12:21 it exposes another wrong view. Paul uses the body analogy again. Imagine what would happen if an eye or a head actually said these things. How would a physical body function?

14. What view of others does this word picture expose? What is the root of this way of thinking? Try to think of at least three options.

15. Devaluing others can happen individually, but it can also happen corporately. How might your particular church elevate some gifts and ministry priorities above others? How might this be unhealthy? What inadvertent effect might this have?

16. In 1 Corinthians 12:22-24 Paul talks about parts that "seem" weaker and "we think" are less honorable. By using this language, he is emphasizing that they are not actually weaker or less honorable. According to these verses what is the right view of these people?

17. Nonetheless, what are some gifts or people groups that are often devalued? Why do we get the idea of value wrong so often?

18. In 1 Corinthians 12:23-24 Paul makes an analogy about a person's unpresentable parts and modesty. How does this analogy inform the way those with less spectacular gifts should be treated?

19. This passage teaches us to value and honor others. Fill in the blanks of this statement for someone you know. "Because you have the gift of _____, you are valuable. I see your giftedness and support you fully. What the Spirit is doing in you completes and complements what the Spirit is doing all through the body." How could you encourage and someone with words like these? How might this help them to serve?

## Is My Body Healthy?

20. In 1 Corinthians 12:25-26 Paul presents the results of honor within the body. This is a picture of unity in the Spirit. For each of these, evaluate your relationships in the church. What might you need to change for these to become reality?

There is no division (v. 25)

We express equal care for all members. (v. 25)

When a member suffers, we willingly enter their pain with them. (v. 26)

When a member is honored, we react with joy—not envy or criticism. (v.26)

21. Finish this lesson by writing a summary of what you have learned. How does a Spirit-filled person view herself/himself and participate in a Spirit-filled church? How do these attitudes and actions display the unity of the Spirit in the presence of diverse people with varied gifts?

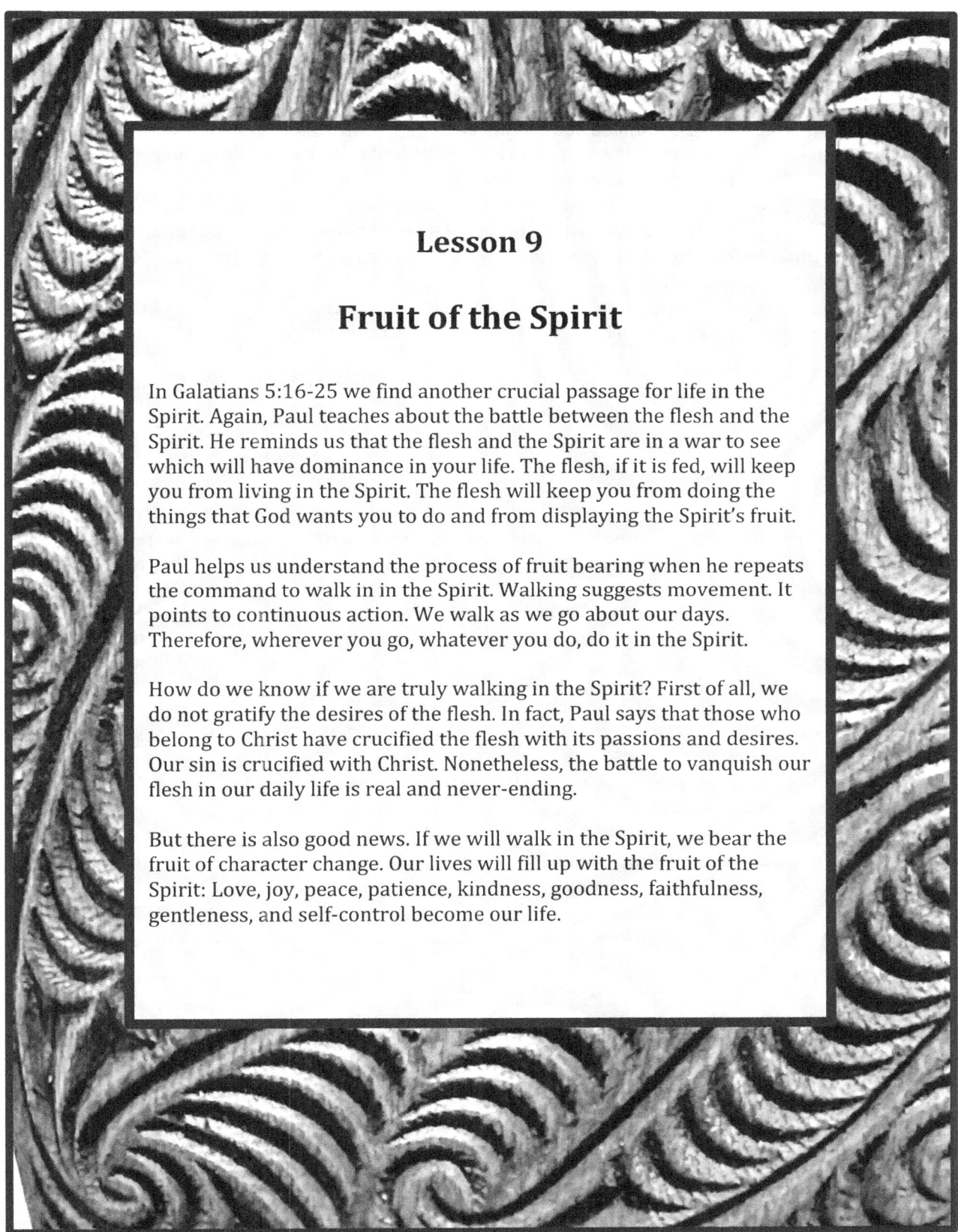

# Lesson 9

# Fruit of the Spirit

In Galatians 5:16-25 we find another crucial passage for life in the Spirit. Again, Paul teaches about the battle between the flesh and the Spirit. He reminds us that the flesh and the Spirit are in a war to see which will have dominance in your life. The flesh, if it is fed, will keep you from living in the Spirit. The flesh will keep you from doing the things that God wants you to do and from displaying the Spirit's fruit.

Paul helps us understand the process of fruit bearing when he repeats the command to walk in in the Spirit. Walking suggests movement. It points to continuous action. We walk as we go about our days. Therefore, wherever you go, whatever you do, do it in the Spirit.

How do we know if we are truly walking in the Spirit? First of all, we do not gratify the desires of the flesh. In fact, Paul says that those who belong to Christ have crucified the flesh with its passions and desires. Our sin is crucified with Christ. Nonetheless, the battle to vanquish our flesh in our daily life is real and never-ending.

But there is also good news. If we will walk in the Spirit, we bear the fruit of character change. Our lives will fill up with the fruit of the Spirit: Love, joy, peace, patience, kindness, goodness, faithfulness, gentleness, and self-control become our life.

## *Daily Exercise Eight*: **Community**

In last week's lesson we embraced several ideas about the Spirit's work in the body of Christ, which is the community of believers. Consider these identity statements distilled from First Corinthians chapter twelve.

- We are the body of Christ, who is the head over all believers. We are people with diverse backgrounds, gifted by the Holy Spirit in various ways to do various ministries all to the glory of God.
- We are a people diligently seeking the Spirit so we each can use the gifts he gives to build up his body. We are a people who values the gifts of others and shows equal care for all.
- We are a people empowered by the Spirit to enter into one another's pain and joy.

For your exercise this week you are going to examine your participation in the life of your local church and ask the Spirit to guide you into deeper Spirit-led fellowship. Contemplate these questions:

How have you sought true fellowship within the structure of your church? Who are your people? What is your commitment to these people? How do you live life with them?

1. If you are having trouble answering these questions, stop here and pray asking the Holy Spirit to lead you to a group of people. As you pray, think of at least two ways you could pursue the goal of being a part of a regular fellowship community. Write these options here and choose one to move toward this week.

2. If you have a community that you love already, consider these prompts and plan an action you can take this week:

How can you love someone in your group this week by entering their joy or pain?

How could you affirm someone's gifting or ministry this week?

How could stir someone up to good works?

How can you open yourself up in greater transparency within your group so that you can receive help when you need it?

## The Flesh

To put our next two lessons in context, read Galatians 5:13-6:10. Paul is teaching about freedom in Christ and how that freedom plays out in a church community. If a believer is going to operate effectively in community—serving, loving, reproving, bearing burdens, sharing—he or she must also walk by the Spirit. By walking in the Spirit and sowing to the Spirit the believer will not be caught up in gratifying the desires of the flesh. In this lesson we will focus on Galatians 5:16-24 and the battle to crucify the flesh and walk in the Spirit to produce the fruit of the Spirit. In our final lesson we will concentrate on Galatians 5:13-15 and 5:25-6:10. These passages that bracket the verses on the fruit of the Spirit, teach us how a life in the Spirit practically plays out in relationships within the church.

1. In Galatians 5:16-17 Paul expresses the same ideas he did in Romans 8. What is the flesh? What is the relationship between the flesh and the Spirit? How does one affect the other?

2. What does Paul mean in Galatians 5:18? (See Galatians 3:11-14.)

3. Paul goes on to list some of the works of the flesh in Galatians 5:19-21. Let's look at these in four groupings. Sort the works of the flesh into these categories:

**Sexual Sin**               **False Worship**               **Relational Sin**               **Sins of Excess**

4. Define any of these sins if you are unsure of their meaning. Then consider your common temptations. Which of these often tempt you? What is your primary struggle with the flesh? How does it help to identify and be aware of your common temptations?

5. What warning does Paul give in Galatians 5:21? How does this apply to believers? How does it apply to those who don't believe?

6. As you consider the seriousness of sin and your common temptations, read 1 Corinthians 6:12-20 and 10:12-13. List the truth that will help you withstand temptation. List the actions to take as you resist temptation.

7. How can you apply these principles—with the help of the Holy Spirit—to help you withstand your common temptations?

## Spiritual Fruit

8. Next Paul lists the fruit of the Spirit in Galatians 5:22-23. Before we study these beautiful fruits notice Galatians 5:24. In what way have those who belong to Christ already crucified the flesh? See Galatians 2:17-21 for Paul's explanation.

9.  The Spirit helps us as we resist sin and seek to live in our already-crucified flesh by faith. However, the Spirit does much more than help us resist sin. He fills us with changed character. Believers can know if they are walking in the Spirit. This list is the test of true Christian character. We will look at these virtues one at a time, but to start your thinking read the list in Galatians 5:22-23 and think about your character. What challenges and affirmations do you see?

**Love** (*agape*) is a self-sacrificing regard and affection for others. It seeks what is best for others. Since God is love, this creates the foundation of all the other virtues. (1 Corinthians 13 gives a longer description of love.) The opposite of loving is being hate-filled, distant, or apathetic.

10. What did Jesus teach about love in Matthew 22:37-40? Consider how these two loves are shown in your life. What evidence of love exists in you?

11. How could you rely on the Holy Spirit to exhibit love for God and neighbor? What is your greatest challenge in loving others. Be specific.

**Joy** (*chara*) is an emotion of great gladness and deep delight. Joy can be distinguished from happiness in that it does not depend on favorable circumstances. The opposite of joy is grumbling, dissatisfaction, sadness, or despondency.

12. Consider Colossians 1:11; 1 Thessalonians 1:6; Hebrews 10:34; and 1 Peter 1:8-9. What gives joy? What part do circumstances play in joy? What part does faith play?

13. Are you a joyful person? Why or why not? What can you do to increase in joy?

**Peace** (*Eirene*) means to live in harmonious relationship; to be free from inner strife. The opposite of peace is relational and inner unrest.

14. Read Philippians 4:4-10. What is the relationship between the peace of God and the God of peace?

15. What can you do to increase in peace according to this passage?

**Patience** (*makrothymia*) is longsuffering under trying circumstances. This is distinguished from mere calmness in waiting by the presence of provocation. The opposite of patience is to be rash or likely to lash out if provoked.

16. Consider 1 Timothy 1:15-16 and Ephesians 4:2-6 for examples of Jesus' patience and a believers' patience. Describe godly patience. How do you react when you are provoked or suffering?

17. How could you engage with the Holy Spirit when you sense your patience is weak or your trials are particularly challenging?

**Kindness** (*chrestotes)* is to be warmhearted or considerate in demeanor. The opposite of kindness is callousness or rudeness.

18. Consider Romans 2:4 as a description of God's kindness. How could you display kindness to others? What attitude and tone best expresses kindness?

19. What affect do you think kindness has on your relationships? Think about family, friends, and work. How can you reach out in kindness?

**Goodness** (*agathosene*) is moral excellence that is actively being lived out by doing good works. The opposite of goodness would be moral failure or disinterest in doing good to others.

20. How can you do good in one of your current circumstances? How can you begin to do it with the Holy Spirit's help?

21. Pray along with 2 Thessalonians 1:11-12 for yourself and for someone you know.

**Faithfulness** (*pistis*) is to be faith-filled and therefore reliable or sincere. The opposite of faithfulness is confusion or unbelief that leads to hypocrisy or being untrustworthy.

22. What are some signs of faithfulness or trustworthiness? How have you experienced a friend or spouse display this characteristic? What effect does faithfulness have on a relationship?

23. What challenges to faithfulness do you face? How can you grow in faithfulness with the Spirit's help?

**Gentleness** (*prautes*) is to be humble and tender, courteous and considerate especially with someone else's weakness. The opposite of gentleness is harshness, anger, or exasperation.

24. Gentleness often comes into play when a correction is needed. (We will learn more about this in our next lesson from Galatians 6:1.) Try to remember a time when you were corrected gently and a time when you were corrected harshly. What did each feel like and what actions did these corrections produce from you?

25. How can you ask the Spirit for gentleness in one of your circumstances? Why would gentleness be the best option?

**Self-control** (*enkrateia*) is to exercise mastery over one's desires and impulses. If love is the motivating foundation of all the fruit of the Spirit, self-control is the means of producing fruit. The opposite of self-control is excess and self-indulgence.

26. As a fruit of the Spirit, self-control is a bit of an oxymoron. How is self-control really Spirit-control? Who powers self-control? What area of life could you submit to the Holy Spirit to move toward mastery of that area?

27. Now that you have walked through the fruits of the Spirit one by one, evaluate your relationship with the Spirit. How has your character changed since you first came to faith? How has your relationship with the Holy Spirit changed over the course of this study? How are you bearing fruit now?

28. Consider the weekly exercises that you have been doing to connect with the Holy Spirit. Which of these has been the most beneficial or born fruit? So far, which ones will you continue as a regular part of your journey with the Holy Spirit?

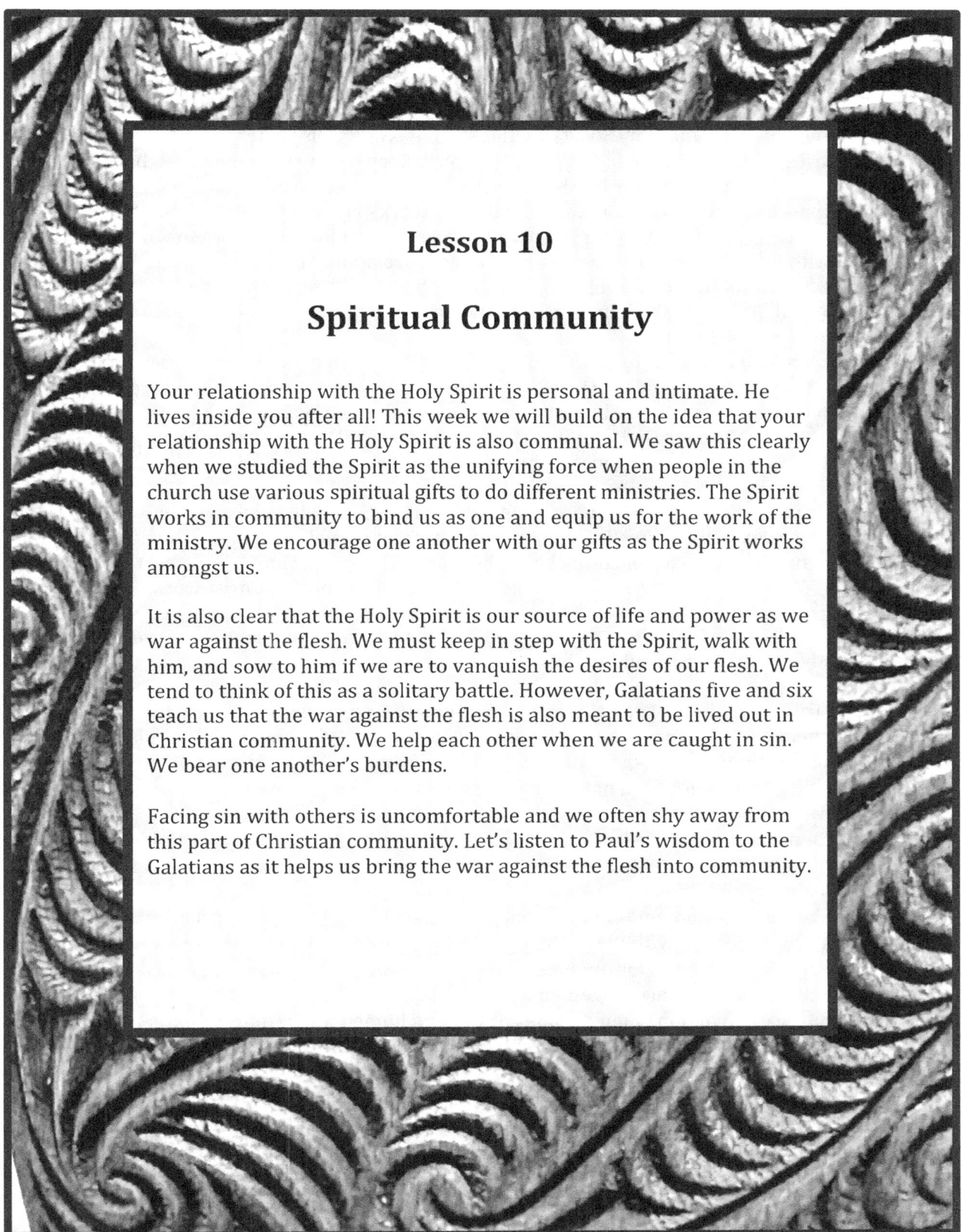

# Lesson 10

# Spiritual Community

Your relationship with the Holy Spirit is personal and intimate. He lives inside you after all! This week we will build on the idea that your relationship with the Holy Spirit is also communal. We saw this clearly when we studied the Spirit as the unifying force when people in the church use various spiritual gifts to do different ministries. The Spirit works in community to bind us as one and equip us for the work of the ministry. We encourage one another with our gifts as the Spirit works amongst us.

It is also clear that the Holy Spirit is our source of life and power as we war against the flesh. We must keep in step with the Spirit, walk with him, and sow to him if we are to vanquish the desires of our flesh. We tend to think of this as a solitary battle. However, Galatians five and six teach us that the war against the flesh is also meant to be lived out in Christian community. We help each other when we are caught in sin. We bear one another's burdens.

Facing sin with others is uncomfortable and we often shy away from this part of Christian community. Let's listen to Paul's wisdom to the Galatians as it helps us bring the war against the flesh into community.

## *Daily Exercise Nine:* Keep in Step

Your relationship with the Holy Spirit is active—not passive. Remember the active metaphors the Bible uses for this relationship: walk in the Spirit, keep in step with the Spirit, be filled with the Holy Spirit, don't grieve the Holy Spirit, and sow to the Spirit. Your relationship with the Holy Spirit began at your salvation when he did the work of regeneration by grace through faith. He indwelt you, affirmed your adoption, and sealed you for the day when you will be glorified with Jesus in heaven. However, your ongoing relationship with the Spirit will depend on your action to submit to his work in you as you obey. It will also depend on his action. It is a combination of both! You abide in him. He works in you.

This week you will concentrate on this combination life. Listen to Paul's encouragement to the Philippian church in Philippians 2:12. "Therefore, my beloved, as you have always obeyed, so now, not only as in my presence but much more in my absence, work out your salvation with fear and trembling, for it is God who works in you, both to will and to work for his good pleasure." You work. God works in you through his Holy Spirit.

Jesus also taught about this combination life in John 15:4-5, "Abide in me, and I in you. As the branch cannot bear fruit by itself, unless it abides in the vine, neither can you unless you abide in me. I am the vine; you are the branches. Whoever abides in me and I in him, he it is that bears much fruit, for apart me you can do nothing." You abide. The Spirit of Christ works.

Your exercise this week is meant to tie together all the exercises you have done over the course of this study and build them into each day this week.

- Start each day with Exercise One: Worshipful Connection. Pray and ask the Holy Spirit to help you keep in step with him as the day goes on. Whatever you have planned for each day, purpose to keep checking in with the triune God in prayer.
- Ask the Holy Spirit for a natural opportunity to ask a question or share some of God's love with someone who doesn't know him yet.
- When you drive or walk or do a mundane task, talk to God about your thoughts or review and meditate on the scripture you have been memorizing. (Or start memorizing Galatians 5:22-24.)
- Take a one-minute mid-morning and mid-afternoon break from work for thankfulness and reconnection with the Spirit. Open your life to him. Be filled.
- Keep your ears open for opportunities to encourage fellow believers and serve them. Text someone an encouragement.
- Embrace conviction when it comes to you and immediately confess your sin. When you face one of your ongoing temptations, stop and pray for power. Sow to the Spirit.
- When you serve in church or some other ministry using your gifts, pray before you begin and ask the Holy Spirit to guide, empower, and work in and through you to display the fruit of the Spirit as you serve.
- Each evening, examine your day with the Lord's help.
- Rejoice in the Spirit and thank him for his presence in your life!

**Free to Serve**

Read Galatians 5:13-6:10. Last week we studied the center section of this passage focusing on the war between flesh and Spirit. We saw that because our flesh with its passions and desires has been crucified with Christ, we have the power to walk in the Spirit. If we walk in the Spirit and deny the flesh, we will bear the fruit of the Spirit. This week we will study the context that brackets this passage. In it we will find that the battle against the flesh is waged in community. We also bear the fruit of the Spirit in community to serve one another, love one another, help one another with sin, bear one another's burdens, share with one another, and do good to one another. As we sow to the Spirit, we reap all these good things and eternal life as well!

1. The letter to the Galatians is all about freedom from the captivity of the Old Testament law. It emphasizes grace for salvation and for the continuing Spirit-led life in Christ. This is the context leading up to the verses we will study this week. According to Galatians 5:13, what were you called to? What opportunity does this give you?

2. What would your life look like if you used your freedom to indulge your flesh? (Think about both personal habits and relationships.)

3. When the Bible uses the phrase "one another" it refers to the community of believers. What does loving service in your church look like in your life? Who benefits from your love and service?

4.  How could what Paul says in Galatians 5:14 be true? Why is love the key to life in Christian community?

5.  What is the warning in Galatians 5:15? How does this relate to loving and serving your community? When have you seen Galatians 5:15 play out?

## Live by the Spirit and Walk by the Spirit

6.  Review Galatians 5:16-24 and summarize its truth in a few sentences.

7.  What admonition does Paul give in Galatians 5:25? What do each of these things mean based on what you have studied over the past ten weeks?

8.  Consider the Holy Spirit's ability to guide your relationships as you live and walk. Describe your process of discerning the Holy Spirit's guiding and correction in relationship. How has this changed over the course of these ten weeks?

9.  In Galatians 5:26 Paul issues another warning. In the context of the war between the flesh and fruit of the Spirit, why this warning? What do each of these things mean?

10. What fruit of the Spirit would be the opposite of each of these?

## Caught in Sin

In Galatians 6:1 Paul addresses an inevitable problem in a body of believers. Sin will overtake us. Even if someone is running from sin or doing their best to withstand temptation, sometimes they will fall to temptation and sin. Notice that Paul says if "anyone" is caught in "any" transgression. This is a very inclusive statement. Helping sinners in community is supposed to be a normal, healthy part of Christian community. The "how" of helping is the tricky part.

11. Who should address another person's sin according to Galatians 6:1? What does "spiritual" mean in the context of Galatians 5:16-25?

12. What is the goal of helping another person recognize their sin in Galatians 6:1? What demeanor is required?

13. What kinds of confrontations about sin would not meet these standards? See Matthew 7:1-5 for more insight.

14. We are tempted to be harsh, judgmental, and even angry when another person sins—especially if they sin against us. The last part of Galatians 6:1 contains a warning for those who seek to help others with their sin. What is the warning and how does it relate to motives for confronting sin?

15. Consider Mathew 18:15-19. What additional steps may be necessary when confronting sin? Why is it important to follow this biblical pattern? What is at stake?

## Bear Burdens

16. In the context of the war between the Spirit and the flesh and helping restore sinners, what does it mean to bear one another's burdens (Galatians 6:2)?

17. What kind of relationship would you need to be aware of another person's burdens and their struggle against sin? How can you build these kinds of relationships? What part does transparency play?

18. How does this fulfil the law of Christ? (See John13:34-35 and Galatians 5:14.)

## Judge Yourself

19. Consider Galatians 6:3-4. What do these verses teach about self-examination? (Read Matthew 7:1-5 again.) What do they teach about comparison? (See 2 Corinthians 10:17-18.)

20. What load is Galatians 6:5 talking about? How is this different than the burden mentioned in Galatians 6:2?

21. In Galatians 6:6 another healthy action of community is commanded. What kind of sharing is this? How do you currently live this out? Think of three new ways you could do this.

**Sow to the Spirit**

22. Describe the pattern of sowing and reaping in Galatians 6:7-8.

23. Why does Paul include the warning, "Do not be deceived. God is not mocked"? What might we be deceived into thinking about the consequences of our life patterns?

24. What are the sure results of sowing to the flesh and sowing to the Spirit? How is this a motivator to enter into the battle against the flesh and for fruit of the Spirit?

25. What additional principle of reaping do you find in Galatians 6:9? When are you tempted to give up or get weary in doing good? What can you do to stay motivated as you sow to the Spirit? (Think about the exercises you have been doing over these ten weeks.)

26. How does Paul conclude this section in Galatians 6:10? Review all the ways he has taught the Galatians to do good in Galatians 5:13-15, 25-26 and Galatians 6:1-10. How can you take this admonition to heart?

27. Take some time to consider your journey with the Holy Spirit over these ten weeks. What have you learned or experienced that will become a part of your regular spiritual life? What do you want to say to the Holy Spirit going forward?

# Study Aids

# Observation

Observation is the process of asking questions of the passage to determine what it says. You are looking for the obvious and the objective. Think: "What does the passage actually say?" not "What do I think or feel about it?" and not "How should I respond to it?" After all, don't we need to understand what a passage is saying before we decide what to think and do about it?

Many observation questions are built into this study. You will find charts to complete and lists to make. Occasionally, in this study you will be asked to "observe" a verse or passage of scripture. The word "observe" is a cue to look at the text objectively. There are many ways to make observations of a passage. Most of them involve reading with a purpose in mind. Here are some prompts that will help you make objective observations:

- Ask who, what, when, where, why, and how of the passage. (Ex. What do I find out about God from this passage? What do I find out about the main character of this story? Who is mentioned in this passage? When did this take place? Etc.)

- Notice what the author says about himself, his audience and God

- Notice time and place

- Make lists of what you observe.

- Look for words that are repeated.

- Look for words that are unfamiliar.

- Look for contrasts.

- Look for comparisons.

- Look for transition words such as: but, and, therefore, since, etc. Then look back to see the context and connections these words are pointing to.

- Look for concepts that are emphasized.

- Make a note of anything you don't understand or would like to know more about.

# Cross-References

Cross-referencing is a useful skill to interpret (discern the meaning of) a text. To cross-reference means to find other places in Scripture that:

- Contain the same words
- Contain similar phrases
- Provide more teaching on the same concepts or topics
- Contain direct quotes from other places in scripture

1. Cross-reference or find other places where a certain word is used.
   - Use the concordance in your study Bible, Blue Letter Bible website, or *Strong's Complete Concordance* to search for the same <u>English</u> words.
   - Use a concordance to find the same Greek or Hebrew words.

2. This leads to a topical study. Both kinds of word studies will help you discover what Scripture says on a given topic.
   - Often searching for opposite words will also help flesh out the meaning of a topic.
   - Searching synonyms will also lead to more teaching on a topic.

3. Cross-reference to find similar phrases.
   - These cross-references are found in the margin of a study Bible. The phrase is marked with a lowercase letter above that phrase in the text and that letter corresponds to a list of references in the margin.
   - These will depend on the scholar who has compiled the cross-references, so it is often wise to consult several study Bibles.
   - Also check the cross-references from the verses that were cross-referenced from your original verse. Following this trail often adds more information to your original search.

4. Cross-reference direct quotes.
   - These are also found in the margin of a study Bible.
   - Look these up to read the quote from its original context.
   - There are many, many Old Testament references in the New Testament. The original context will help you understand the new usage.
   - Jesus often quoted the Old Testament.

# Word Study

The Bible is an ancient book originally written in ancient languages: Hebrew, Aramaic, and Greek. The first translations of the Bible were from these original languages into Latin. Throughout history a series of translations have been made into other commonly spoken languages such as English.

Modern translations (such as the NASB, ESV, and NIV) translate from the earliest documents of the original languages into the English words we use today. Language is fluid, so when you read your modern translation, you are reading the work of many men making their best linguistic effort to convey what the text said in the original. Very little is "lost in translation," so you can be confident in the Bible you have in your hands.

That being said, often we understand less than we think we do, and are unsure of the meaning even of English words. In addition, there are often nuances in the original languages that don't get captured completely by English. You can discover much by doing a basic word study.

What words should you look up?

- Any word that you don't understand
- Any word that seems critical to the meaning of the passage
- Repeated key words
- Words that you wouldn't use in normal conversation that seem especially unique to the Bible (like "grace" or "blessed")
- Places or people that are not familiar

# Word Study Step by Step

**Step1:**
**Look up your word in the alphabetical listing of an exhaustive concordance.**
Use an exhaustive concordance keyed to the translation you are using. *Strong's Exhaustive Concordance* is keyed to the King James Version, but you can access others keyed to the version of the Bible you are using. These are available in book form or for free online. Blue Letter Bible is a popular online concordance/study tool: www.blueletterbible.org. It is also available for free as an app for your mobile device. Literal Word is another free word study app. If you use the online versions, you will use their search engines and procedures rather than this "step-by-step" which is designed for traditional references. Blue Letter Bible has tutorials on the site, or you can view a tutorial I made here:
https://envolvemedia.adobeconnect.com/_a984979381/blbtutorial

**Step2:**
**Scan the list of references to find the verse that contained the word you are studying.**
There are often several Hebrew or Greek words that are translated into one English word, so it is important to locate your reference.

**Step 3:**
**Make a note of the number that the concordance has assigned to that particular word.**

**Step 4:**
**Using that number, go to the numerical listing in the "dictionary" section in the back of the concordance and find the Greek or Hebrew word that corresponds to the number.**

**Step 5:**
**Write the Greek or Hebrew word and make notes on the definition found in that "dictionary."**

**Step 6:**
**Look up the English word numerically or alphabetically in an expository Bible dictionary.**
*Vine's Expository Dictionary* is a good basic resource. Make sure you are looking at the definition for the Greek (or Hebrew) keyed word from your passage. Make notes of what the dictionary says for that Greek or Hebrew word in your particular passage. Spiros Zodhiates' *Complete Word Study Dictionary* is also a great resource for the New Testament. Its entries are listed by the Strong's concordance number. For Hebrew, *The Complete Word Study Dictionary: Old Testament* is a good resource.

**Step 7:**
**Now look up the word in an English dictionary.**
Often there are multiple definitions for a single English word. You must use context to determine which definition is applicable to your passage.

**Step 8:**
**Use all the information you have gathered to define the word you are studying.**
Often it is helpful to use all your gathered information to paraphrase the definition. This will stretch you, but it will help clarify the meaning for you.
**Other helpful uses of the Exhaustive Concordance:**

1.  Note all the other places that particular Greek (or Hebrew) word is used. (Is it a common or uncommon word?)

2.  Look up some of the other places that word is used. Often those references, in context, will also give you insight into the usage in your passage. Using blueletterbible.org makes this easy.

3.  These references will also help you cross-reference the full counsel of scripture on that topic. You can make a list of your findings on a particular topic.

4.  Make special note of the places where the author of your particular book has used that word. Usage is often very consistent within an author's writing.

5.  Note what other Greek (or Hebrew) words are translated into the same English word. See if you can make distinctions between these passages and meanings.

# Bibliography

Boice, James Montgomery. *Romans: The Reign of Grace*. Vol. 2. Grand Rapids, MI: Baker Book House, 1991–.

Carson, D. A. *The Gospel according to John*. The Pillar New Testament Commentary. Leicester, England; Grand Rapids, MI: Inter-Varsity Press; W.B. Eerdmans, 1991.

Carson, D.A., *Showing the Spirit A Theological Exposition on 1 Corinthians 12-14*, Grand Rapids, MI: Baker Book House Company, 1987.

Ciampa, Roy E. and Rosner, Brian S. *The First Letter to the Corinthians The Pillar New Testament Commentary*. Grand Rapids, MI; Cambridge, U.K.: William B. Eerdmans Publishing Company, 2010.

Fee, Gordon, *The First Epistle to the Corinthians The New International Commentary on the New Testament*. Grand Rapids, MI: William B. Erdmans Publishing Company, 1987

Grudem, Wayne, *Systematic Theology, An Introduction to Biblical Doctrine.* Leicester, England: Inter-Varsity Press and Grand Rapids, MI: Zondervan, 1994

Lenski, R. C. H., *The Interpretation of St. Paul's First and Second Epistle to the Corinthians*, Minneapolis, MN: Augsburg Publishing House, 1963, 501–502.

MacArthur Jr., John F. and Mayhue, Richard, *Biblical Doctrine A Systematic Summary of Bible Truth.* Wheaton, IL: Crossway, 2017.

MacArthur Jr., John F., *1 Corinthians MacArthur New Testament Commentary*. Chicago: Moody Press, 1984.

MacArthur, John F., Jr. *John 12–21*. MacArthur New Testament Commentary. Chicago, IL: Moody Publishers, 2008.

MacArthur, John F., Jr. *Romans*. MacArthur New Testament Commentary. Chicago: Moody Press, 1991.

Rydelnik, Michael and Vanlaningham, Michael, *The Moody Bible Commentary,* Chicago, IL: Moody Press 2014.

Sproul, R. C. *Who Is the Holy Spirit?*. Vol. 13 of *The Crucial Questions Series*. Orlando, FL: Reformation Trust, 2012.

Thiselton, Anthony C., *The First Epistle to the Corinthians: A Commentary on the Greek Text*, New International Greek Testament Commentary, Grand Rapids, MI: W.B. Eerdmans, 2000, 948.

Walvoord, John F. and Zuck, Roy B., Dallas Theological Seminary, *The Bible Knowledge Commentary: An Exposition of the Scriptures*. Wheaton, IL: Victor Books, 1985.

Wilder, Jim and Hendricks, Michel, *The Other Half of Church: Christian Community, Brain Science, and Overcoming Spiritual Stagnation.* Chicacgo, IL: Moody Press 2020

Zodhiates, Spiros, *The Complete Word Study Dictionary: New Testament*, Chattanooga, TN: AMG Publishers, 1993.

*The Holy Bible: English Standard Version*. Wheaton, IL: Standard Bible Society, 2016.

Made in the USA
Las Vegas, NV
11 February 2025

17874990R10072